The Peedie

Orkney

Guide Book

D1336082

by Charles Tait

4th Edition (2nd revised)

ISBN 9781909036000

The Peedie Orkney Guide Book

4th Edition (revised 2017)
Published by Charles Tait
Kelton, St Ola, Orkney KW15 1TR
Tel 01856 873738
charles.tait@zetnet.co.uk   charles-tait.co.uk

Text, design and layout © copyright Charles Tait 2017
Photographs © copyright Charles Tait 1975-2017
Old Photographs from Charles Tait collection
Printing by Martins, Berwick-upon-Tweed
OS maps reproduced from Ordnance Survey mapping with permission
of the Controller of HMSO, © Crown Copyright Reserved 100035677

This book is dedicated to my aunt, Margaret C Tait (1918-1999)
Cinematographer, Poet, Artist and Inspiration

ISBN 9781909036000

Aerial view of Brodgar, the Loch of Stenness and the Hoy Hills

The Peedie

ORKNEY

Guide Book

by Charles Tait

CONTENTS

Welcome to Orkney

The Ring of Brodgar, West Mainland

WELCOME TO ORKNEY, where there is much to see and do. This guide is designed to help visitors find and appreciate the main sites of interest on the Mainland and other islands. The rich archaeological heritage is one of the prime attractions. The soft green and fertile landscape, beautiful beaches, spectacular cliffs, abundant wildlife and above all the friendly people are equally important in making up "Orkney".

The archipelago lies just north of mainland Scotland at 59°N. It comprises over 70 islands of which 17 or 18 are inhabited by about 21,000 people. The first written reference to the islands is by Pytheas the Greek from about 325BC, but they have been inhabited for at least 6,000 years. The timeline from prehistory through historical times to the 21st century is continuous, making the division between past and present at times hard to discern.

Attractions Perhaps most famous for its exceptionally well preserved Neolithic monuments, some of which now enjoy World Heritage status, Orkney has a wealth of visitor attractions. These range from archaeological sites, local museums, the Highland Park Distillery and St Magnus Cathedral, to a diverse array of craft workshops and shops selling attractive local goods. Wildlife, especially birds, is another feature of Orkney not to be missed, whatever the season.

Geology The Old Red Sandsto rocks results in fertile agricultur land, most of which is used raise Orkney's renowned gras fed beef cattle. Moorland ar spectacular coastal fringes, ma it a haven for many species birds in every season, while spring and summer wild flowe are abundant.

Climate The maritime clima combined with the relative warm Atlantic Ocean, make tl climate equable, with snow ar frost rare in winter. Equally, tl temperature rarely exceeds 20° summer. Situated at the mee ing point of the North Sea ar Atlantic Ocean the islands a surrounded by waters abunda in fish and shellfish, adding to tl wide variety of locally produce quality foods.

Arrival Whether one arrives l air or sea at Kirkwall or by sea Stromness, St Margaret's Hor or Burwick, Orkney presents strong contrast to the Highland Both towns are dominated l their winding main streets ar harbours, while Kirkwall has tl imposing 12th century St Magnt Cathedral.

Both towns have excellent shop hotels and eating places, as we

Yesnaby Castle at midsummer, Thrift in foreground

interesting museums and make ...od bases from which to explore ...e rest of Orkney. Even on the ...ortest of visits there are several ...ust see" sites.

...uggested Starting Points are ...e Orkney Museum or the ...ighland Park Visitor Centre, ...th its excellent audiovisual, in ...irkwall. A tour of the West ...ainland taking in Maeshowe, ...e Ring of Brodgar, the Standing ...ones of Stenness and Skara ...ae is essential. If time permits ...ere are many more places which ...n be visited in a day.

...lands On a longer stay it is ...rongly suggested that a visit ...ould be made to at least one ...the other inhabited islands, all ...which are easily accessible by ...rry or aircraft. Each island has ...character all of its own and all ...ve interesting places to visit as ...ell as accommodation and shops.

...rdnance Survey Maps A good ...ap is a great help in all such ...sits and VisitOrkney produces ...useful one which also includes ...etland. The Ordnance Survey ...50,000 Landranger Series cov-...s Orkney in three sheets, while ...e 1:25,000 Explorer Series has ...ve sheets. These maps, or their ...gital equivalent, are recom-...ended for all serious explorers.

St Magnus Cathedral in Kirkwall dates from 1137

Short-eared Owl

Grey Seal pup

...ffins and other seabirds come ashore to breed in summer

ORKNEY COUNTRYSIDE CODE

We are justly proud of our historic sites, wildlife and environment. Please help ensure that future visitors may enjoy them as much as you by observing these guidelines:

1. Always use stiles and gates and close gates after you.
2. Always ask permission before entering agricultural land.
3. Keep to paths and take care to avoid fields of grass and crops.
4. Do not disturb livestock.
5. Take your litter away with you and do not light fires.
6. Do not pollute water courses or supplies.
7. Never disturb nesting birds.
8. Do not pick wild flowers or dig up plants.
9. Drive and park with due care and attention - do not obstruct or endanger others.
10. Always take care near cliffs - particularly with children and pets.
11. Walkers should take adequate clothes, wear suitable footwear and tell someone of their plans.
12. Above all please respect the life of the countryside - leave only footprints, take only photographs and pleasant memories.

Notice: While most of the sites of interest are open to the public and have marked access, many are on private land. Right of access is not implied, and if in doubt it is always polite to ask. Not all roads and tracks are rights of way.

NEOLITHIC ORKNEY There is a wealth of Neolithic sites to visit, of which Maeshowe, the Standing Stones of Stenness, the Ness of Brodgar, the Ring of Brodgar and Skara Brae are the most spectacular. The great chambered cairn of Maeshowe is the largest and grandest of its type. All of these ancient precincts date from the early third millennium BC.

Maeshowe entrance passage lit up by the winter solstice sunset

Together these monuments form the UNESCO World Heritage Site, "*The Heart of Neolithic Orkney*". They are situated in the heart of the West Mainland, surrounded by farmland and near the lochs of Stenness and Harray, in turn ringed by heather-covered low hills. There is a timeless and spacious feel to this landscape as a result of the dramatic confluence of sky, water and land.

Skara Brae The Neolithic village of Skara Brae lies on the shore of the Bay of Skaill. Its well preserved 5,000 year old houses give a very good impression of life then, having been protected under sand dunes for several thousand years, before being revealed by storms.

The Ring of Brodgar is a spectacular henge monument over 100m across

There is a Visitor Centre at Skara Brae with a museum, replica house and a shop. Tormiston Mill, next to Maeshowe, also has a shop and interpretive display. The nearby excavation at the Ness of Brodgar is an essential visit during summer. Barnhouse Village, the Watchstone and the Ring of Bookan are nearby.

The Neolithic site at the Ness of Brodgar is under excavation

Skara Brae Neolithic village was rediscovered after a storm in the 19ᵗʰ centu

There are many other fascinating monuments and sites of interest, ranging from the Neolithic to the 20ᵗʰ century, which can be visited all over Orkney. Every parish and island has something different and special left by the people who inhabited the countryside during the last six millennia.

ochs The continuity of settlement in Orkney is well demonstrated by the Broch of Gurness. With its surrounding settlement and ramparts, this is one of the best examples of over a possible 100 such structures in Orkney. It dates from the late Iron Age. The settlement was occupied for hundreds of years at least until early Norse times. Pictish houses can be viewed here.

Broch of Gurness aerial view showing the broch and settlement

cts and Vikings The Brough of Birsay is a tidal island off the northwest of the Mainland. It is the site of both Pictish and Viking settlements, with secular and ecclesiastic remains. These include Norse houses and a well preserved church. In the nearby village of The Palace, the ruins of the 16th century Earl's Palace provide a gaunt reminder of the more recent past, while St Magnus Kirk is built on the site of a much older church.

Brough of Birsay aerial view showing Viking Age settlement ruins

Magnus Cathedral The 12th century St Magnus Cathedral in Kirkwall was built by the Norse Earl, Rognvald Kolson, in honour of his murdered uncle, Earl Magnus Erlendson. It dominates the town, and its warm coloured Old Red Sandstone, unmarked by pollution, makes the building especially attractive. The interior is particularly impressive and well proportioned.

St Magnus Cathedral dates from 1137

alian Chapel During WWII several hundred Italian prisoners of war worked on the construction of the Churchill Barriers. This was to defend the eastern approaches to Scapa Flow from German seaward attack. During their time here, the prisoners built the Italian Chapel in their camp on Lamb Holm. This unusual and charming surviving artefact of war stands now as a symbol of hope and peace.

The Italian Chapel was built during WWII by Italian POWs

Nature and Environment

Natural Environment

As well as the huge array of ancient and more recent monuments, Orkney also has a rich and interesting natural environment. The combination of fertile farmland with a great variety of other habitats makes it a very good place for wildlife, especially birds. There are cliffs, beaches, marshes, moors and maritime heath as well as sheltered bays, small islands and lochs, all of which attract a variety of different species, depending on the season and weather.

Rough seas at Skipi Geo, Birsay

The many superb beaches, dramatic cliffs and inland paths provide wonderful opportunities for walking. Whether just a stroll along the Bay of Skaill or Aikerness after visiting Skara Brae or the Broch of Gurness, or one of the many more adventurous walks, Orkney will never fail to please. The islands are also great for cycling, as the hills are not steep, and the side roads are (mostly) quiet.

The Old Man of Hoy is one of Orkney's "trade marks"

The predominant daytime colours here are the greens, blues and browns of grass, water, moor and sky. The hues vary with the season and are particularly vibrant in summer, but more muted in other seasons. Orkney is also famous for its sunsets and its long hours of daylight in summer. The Northern Lights or Aurora Borealis are occasionally seen, usually on a dark moonless winter night. Skies are generally not polluted by light, so the stars and planets are easily observed.

There are many superb beaches in Orkney, like Grobust on Westray

Aikerness beach in Evie overlooks Eynhallow Sound

The Orkney climate is much influenced by the sea, which varies in temperature by only a few degrees over the year. This ensures that winters are mild, but also that summers are never hot. The weather is very variable, and it is possible to have every season in a day.

The combination of constantly changing weather and day length make for a huge variety of lighting conditions. This makes Orkney a paradise for artists, photographers and lovers of the landscape in all seasons. Thus there is no "best" time to visit. Just wait a few minutes and everything will be different.

There are many good locations for observing wildlife, including several RSPB Reserves. During the summer many thousands of birds breed in Orkney. The cliff colonies of seabirds are especially impressive at Marwick Head in Birsay, and Noup Head in Westray. Waders, waterfowl and several species of raptor are also common. Both Grey and Common Seals, as well as Otters also breed here.

Maritime Heath, for example, on Papay and on Rousay is home to the diminutive and endemic *Primula scotica*. They are also a favourite nesting site for Terns and Arctic Skuas, while the Heather Moorland on the hills is home to Hen Harriers, Merlins and Short-eared Owls as well as many species of Waders. Oystercatchers, Curlews, Dunlin, Redshanks, and Golden Plovers are particularly abundant.

Orkney is also a fine place to see migrants and winter visitors such as Great Northern Divers, Long-tailed Ducks, Goldeneye, Iceland Gulls and other species. The Peedie Sea, harbours at Kirkwall and Stromness and the lochs in the vicinity of the Standing Stones are good places to look for these birds. The beach at Scapa, near Kirkwall, is perhaps the handiest to reach of many, while the sheltered waters round the Churchill Barriers are usually attractive to Great Northern Divers and seaducks.

Aurora borealis from Wideford Hill in autumn

Midwinter sunset at the Loch of Stenness

Puffins are one of the many bird species which can be seen in Orkney

Orkney is home to a large number of Grey Seals which pup in autumn

Kirkwall Harbour Basin

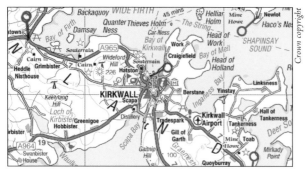

Crown copyright

KIRKWALL (ON *Kirkjuvagr*, Church Bay), as the main settlement in Orkney, is a good starting point for a visit to the islands. It is first mentioned in the *Orkneyinga Saga*. It was the dwelling place of Earl Rognvald Brusison about 1035, who built a church, dedicated to King Olav of Norway there.

Later, the town developed around the Cathedral, and became the administrative and commercial centre. Its access to the North Isles, central position and sheltered harbour in the Peedie Sea, which was then much larger, made it an obvious location.

Today the winding main street still follows the shape of the original settlement. Many of the fine old houses with end-on gables date from the 16th to 18th centuries. Narrow lanes run off the Street which has many attractive shops. At Broad Street it opens into the expanse of the grass covered Kirk Green in front of St Magnus Cathedral.

The harbour front is the scene of much activity with ferries, fishing boats and, in summer, cruise ships. Over the last 200 years the pier has greatly expanded, but it still retains much of its charm. The marina is home to pleasure craft and is visited by many yachts in the summer. Occasionally one or more tall ships lends a taste of nostalgia to the scene.

Orkney Museum is located in Tankerness House, parts of which date from the 15th century. This is an excellent starting point from which to gain an insight into Orkney's rich past. Exhibits range from The Neolithic Age right up to the present. Themed collections change annually and artists' exhibitions are also held.

Tankerness House Garden, behind the museum, is a pleasant place for a sheltered seat on a nice day. St Magnus Cathedral is across the road, and makes a suitable finale to a visit, with its peaceful interior and warm coloured sandstone.

Palaces The nearby Bishop's and Earl's Palaces date from Norse and Scottish times. The former was first built at the same time as the Cathedral, and was when King Haakon Haakonson died in 1263 after the "Battle" of Largs. The "Moosie Tower" was built during the 16th century.

The Earl's Palace was built by the notorious Earl Patrick Stewart in the early 17th century, but was only briefly occupied. It was roofless by 1750. Patrick was executed for treason in 1615 and so had little time to enjoy his palace which has been described as a Scottish Renaissance Masterpiece.

Shopping The Kirkwall Street including Bridge, Albert, Broad and Victoria Streets has a wide selection of interesting independent shops. This is a good place to seek out inspirational local crafts, souvenirs or presents. They stock knitwear, Orkney jewellery, local crafts and books, as well as many other home produced items. There is plenty of opportunity for retail therapy.

The Bishop's and Earl's Palaces

The Big Tree in Albert Street

Kirkwall is dominated by the 12ᵗʰ century St Magnus Cathedral

n addition there is a good selection of Orkney drink products including Highland Park and Scapa Malt Whisky, Kirkjuvagr and Deerness Gin. The Orkney and Swannay Breweries produce distinctive ranges of ales. Orkney cheese, Orkney oatcakes, fresh and smoked fish and shellfish of various kinds and of course the famous Orkney Beef are all on sale locally.

Eating Out There is a wide choice of establishments around Kirkwall offering food and drink. These range from first class restaurants to chip shops and authentic Indian and Italian eateries. All offer local produce and friendly service. Some of the pubs feature live music, while The Reel, on Broad Street, is run by the famous Wrigley Sisters.

Scapa Beach is 2km (1.5mi) south of the town and makes

a fine circular walk. There are expansive views over Scapa Flow from here. This is a good place for bird watching at all times of year, especially for waders and sea ducks - even occasionally cetaceans.

Wideford Hill is a fine vantage point from which to gain an overall impression of Orkney. Just to the west of Kirkwall on the

Old Finstown Road, the summit (226m) can be reached by footpath or by road (8km, 5mi return). From here there is a panoramic view of most of the North and South Isles, East and West Mainland and Scapa Flow. Scotland can be seen in the far distance to the south. This is a fine vantage point for sunrises and sunsets.

Kirkwall Harbour Basin and the RNLI Lifeboat

Tankerness House on Broad Street is the home of the Orkney Museum

KIRKWALL
St Magnus Cathedral
Orkney Museum
Earls' Palace
Bishop's Palace
The Harbour
Peedie Sea
The Street - Shopping
Highland Park Visitor Centre
Wideford Hill
Scapa Beach
Scapa Distillery Visitor Centre
Evening Entertainment
Kirkwall Ba' Game

St Magnus Cathedral

St Magnus Cathedral nave from the west door

St Magnus Cathedral remains a symbol of the 600 year Norse sovereignty over Orkney, and of the power and wealth of the Norse Earldom. For over 875 years it has dominated Kirkwall.

In 1103 the cousins Magnus Erlendson and Haakon Paulson succeeded to the Earldom. At first all went well, but by c.1117, disputes had arisen, and it was agreed to meet on Egilsay on 16th April. The plan was that each Earl was to take only two ships, but Haakon arrived with eight and in an uncompromising mood.

Soon it was resolved to execute the rival Earl.

Eventually Haakon's cook, Lifolf, was ordered to kill Magnus, which he did by cleaving his skull. A cenotaph now stands on the spot where this act is said to have taken place. The roofless 12th century St Magnus Church on Egilsay is one of many churches named after the martyred Earl.

Magnus was buried at Christ's Church in Birsay; soon prayers were being said to him, and miraculous cures were claimed to be taking place. Later, Earl Haakon made a pilgrimage to Rome, and on his return had the now ruined St Nicholas Round Church built at the Bu in Orphir, in c.1122.

He was succeeded by his son Paul, who was deposed in 1136 by Magnus' nephew Rognvald Kolson. Rognvald had vowed to build *"a stone minster at Kirkwall and to dedicate it to Earl Magnus the Holy"*. In 1137 on St Lucia Day (13th December) he is said to have laid the foundation stone. Today a festival is held on the first Saturday of December to celebrate St Lucia and the start of Christmas.

Much of the finance came from local farmers under pressure from the Earl. Durham masons were drafted in to supervise construction work. The church was consecrated about 1150 when Magnus' remains were transferred to a shrine in the east end of the building. This was in the apse, which was later extended to form the present St Rognvald's Chapel.

The choir was lengthened in the 13th century, and the nave extended also so that by the 14th century the Cathedral was more or less complete. Over the centuries it was allowed to fall into disrepair, but extensive restoration works have been carried out since the late 19th century. This work continues today.

12th century consecration cross carving

St Magnus Church, Egilsay

St Magnus Cathedral is built from Old Red Sandstone, said to have been quarried at nearby Head of Holland, and also on Eday. It lends the slightly austere exterior a warm look, which is particularly apparent in early morning or evening light. The varied use of colour is very effective.

The interior of the Cathedral is about 69m long and 30m across the transepts, while only 5m separates the pillars in the nave. Despite this, the overall impression is of space and balance with the attractive colours of the stone giving a very welcoming feel.

The Cathedral belongs to the people of Kirkwall and Orkney, having been largely financed by them over the centuries. It is the principal venue of the annual St Magnus Festival, whose founders include the composer, Sir Peter Maxwell Davies, and the Stromness poet, George MacKay Brown.

St Magnus Centre, the former church hall, is continued evidence of the strong role that the Cathedral continues to play in the Orkney community. It has a cafe open in summer, meeting rooms and a large hall. Weddings, conferences talks and other gatherings take place here. It also offers fine views of the east end of St Magnus Cathedral over the graveyard.

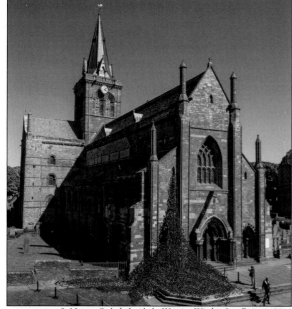
St Magnus Cathedral with the Weeping Window Installation in 2016

St Magnus stained glass window

West nave stained glass window

Memorial to the 19th century Arctic explorer, John Rae

HMS "Royal Oak" memorial

Malting Floo

Drying Malted Barley in the Kil

Bonded Warehou

Highland Park Distillery

DISTLLERIES & BREWERIES

Orkney has a growing range of establishments producing malt whisky, artisan gin, craft ales and even wine. All have actual or online shops and most offer tours.

The Highland Park Distillery, the most northerly in Scotland, was founded in 1798, at a house belonging to Magnus Eunson, a smuggler and illicit distiller, but also a Church Officer. On hearing that the Excisemen were after him, he removed all his casks from the kirk to his house, covered

Lomond Still at Scapa Distillery

them with a coffin lid and a white cloth and called the congregation together. When the customs arrived he was conducting a funeral service, and a whispered "smallpox!" sent them packing.

Highland Park Visitor Centre on the southeastern edge of the town offers visits to the distillery. The shop stocks many items, mostly branded, and the full range of Highland Park Malt Whisky, in many ages and expressions.

Scapa Distillery was established in 1885; it bottles all of its production as a single malt, with various expressions available. First fill American Oak casks make it *bright, sweet, silky and smooth*. A rare Lomond-style still is used alongside a conventional one.

Scapa Distillery Visitor Centre is off the A964 overlooking Scapa Bay about 3km (1.5mi) southwest of Kirkwall. Tours are run all year. The distillery is part of the Pernod Ricard Group.

Kirkjuvagr Gin - A Myth in th Making. *"We discovered a loca legend about Angelica brought t the islands by Norsemen centurie ago, which can still be found today This very Angelica is now one o our defining ingredients, comple menting a blend of local botanical including Ramanas Rose, Burne Rose and Borage. Uniquely, we'v also used Orkney Bere Barley our recipe.*

We handcraft our gin in sma batches using traditional coppe stills in a process defined by passion

Scapa Distille

commitment and attention to detail. After all, the Vikings didn't mess around. Nor do we."

Deerness Distillery was founded by Stuart and Adelle Brown to make truly handcrafted spirits and liqueurs. It can accommodate a number of stills which will be used to distil artisanal gin, vodka and rum. The entire process is carried out by hand. The distillery also has a range of merchandise sourced and produced locally. A shop and licensed café will allow visitors to sample the spirits and liqueurs and enjoy teas, coffees and local produce.

Orkney Brewery is based in the former Quoyloo School. *"There is no better place to learn about the history of brewing. Kids will love dressing up in Victorian school uniform on the childrens' tour. Adults will enjoy finding out how our wonderful, hand-crafted beers are made.*

The gift shop offers some of our products and merchandise, as well as a range of local crafts and produce. And you can sample our creations in the Tasting Hall Café where we serve a selection of local specialities.

We create fine hand-crafted ales, using traditional methods. Only the finest ingredients and purest Orcadian water can create these outstanding, full-of-flavour ales. "

Orkney Brewery

Kirkjuvagr Gin

Swannay Brewery is located on the northwesterly tip of the Mainland. *"Based in an old farmstead we're in a unique location: showered in spray from the Atlantic Ocean in the winter and surrounded by fertile farmland. With 25 years' brewing experience Rob Hill knew exactly what the first beer needed to be: Scapa Special, our flagship pale ale that still accounts for around a third of all we brew today.*

Careful not to get carried away with growth for the sake of growth, our absolute main focus is still making

Swannay Brewery - Scapa Special
the best beer we possibly can; it's what Rob did in the early days to get the business going and it is what will ensure the brewery's longevity."

Orkney Wine Company is based on Lamb Holm near the Italian Chapel. *"All our wines and liqueurs are made in the traditional way using fruit, flowers and vegetables, which are fermented whole resulting in high levels of anti-oxidants and maximum flavour. Only the finest natural ingredients are used, with as much as possible grown in Orkney."*

Deerness Distillery

Orkney Wine Company

Midsummer sunset at the Ring of Brodgar

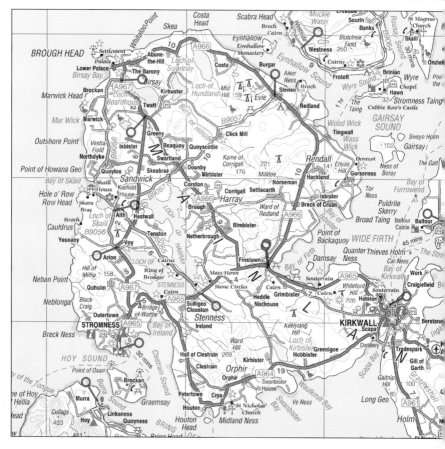

WEST MAINLAND The West Mainland includes *"The Heart of Neolithic Orkney"*, a designated UNESCO World Heritage Site, which includes Maeshowe, the Standing Stones of Stenness, the Ness of Brodgar, Ring of Brodgar, Skara Brae, and parts of the surrounding area.

There is a strong argument for the whole of Orkney to be a World Heritage Site in view of its unique natural and cultural heritage, however for now the designation is cultural only. The West Mainland encompasses, in a small and accessible area, most of what is best about the archipelago.

Aside from archaeology, there are many other places of interest. These include dramatic coastline such as at Yesnaby, Marwick Head and the Brough of Birsay. Orkney also has exceptional beaches; examples are Warebeth, the Bay of Skaill, Birsay, Aikerness and Waulkmill.

"Grooved Ware" pottery

Apart from the main Neolithic sites, there are many others to visit. These include Neolithic chambered cairns at Bookan, Unstan, Cuween and Wideford Hill. The Broch of Gurness is the best preserved of many such Iron Age sites. There are Pictish and Norse ruins on the Brough of Birsay, and a 16th century Earl's Palace in the Village.

Ancient fossils at Yesnaby

Aerial view of the heart of Orkney

Nature For birdwatchers and botanists, the huge variety of habitats ensures a wide range of species to see at any season, while anglers have a choice of several lochs on which to try their skills and luck. Walkers will also find a diverse selection of interesting routes, coastal or inland, easy or more strenuous. There is much to do in the West Mainland.

The Ring of Brodgar

The Farm Museums at Corrigall and Kirbuster, the Click Mill and Boardhouse Mill, all date from the 19ᵗʰ century. Skaill House, next to Skara Brae is a restored laird's home full of interesting artefacts.

Stromness has its internationally acclaimed Pier Arts Centre and a delightful small museum, reached through narrow, winding streets.

The sheltered harbour was called *Hamnavoe* by the Norse.

Orphir offers fine views over the great natural harbour of Scapa Flow, once home to the British Fleet, and last resting place of the WWI German Grand Fleet. The St Nicholas Round Kirk is Norse, and was built by Earl Haakon in atonement for his murder of Earl, later St, Magnus.

WEST MAINLAND
WORLD HERITAGE SITE
Skara Brae, Ring of Brodgar, Ness of Brodgar, Barnhouse, Stones of Stenness, Maeshowe
OTHER PLACES TO VISIT
Brough of Birsay
Yesnaby
Marwick Head
Broch of Gurness
Skaill House
Farm Museums & Mills
Stromness
Orphir
Lochs of Harray & Stenness
Scapa Flow
Craft Workshops
Galleries

Hut 1 with its stone dresser, beds, central fireplace and sea view

SKARA BRAE The 5,000 year-old Neolithic village of Skara Brae was buried under sand dunes at the Bay of Skaill, in the West Mainland, until 1850, when it was revealed during a violent storm. The houses are so intact that it is easy to imagine their inhabitants going about their lives. The site was occupied from about 3100BC to about 2600BC, and consists of at least six dwellings, all joined together by a "street" and buried in a mound of midden except for the freestanding "workshop".

The huts are well constructed with drains, (perhaps) damp-proof courses, stone dressers, beds, cupboards and tanks. There are even cells with drains which might be toilets. All are quite similar in design and vary from about 6m x 6m to 4m x 4m. The roofs may have been supported by whalebone or driftwood rafters. They would have been covered with hides, turf and perhaps with straw or reed thatch, all held down with heather or straw ropes.

Hut 8 appears to have been the workshop, with evidence of stone working, and pottery making. *"Grooved Ware"* pottery was found along with many bone and stone tools as well as jewellery items made from bone and shells.

The people were stock farmers who reared cattle, sheep, som pigs and deer. They also fishe in the sea, which would ha been prolific with Cod, Haddoc Saithe and many species of shel fish. They also grew Bere Barley

Due to the small amount of fli in Orkney, chert was served t make cutting tools. Bone wa much utilised, but wood wa not well preserved, though pre sumably it would also have bee extensively used. Although ther was no evidence of textile makin, many possible leather workir tools were found, suggesting tha the people may have been quit well dressed, perhaps using skir and furs.

Panoramic view of Skara Brae with the Bay of Skaill in the background

Aerial view of Skara Brae

replica of hut 7

Skara Brae is contemporary with the other Orkney Neolithic monuments. It is so far the best preserved village to have been found and the only one which can be visited, apart from the houses at Knap of Howar on Papa Westray and the settlement at Barnhouse in Stenness. The fact that it is so impressively designed and built suggests that its inhabitants were well settled in Orkney and not newcomers.

Hut 7 - now not visible to the public

carved stone object - possibly a bull's head with geometric carvings

The "Street"

NEOLITHIC TIMELINE	
BC	
c.3600	Knap of Howar oldest *Unstan Ware* pottery
c.3300	Barnhouse earliest Oldest Ness of Brodgar
c.3200	Earliest dates Skara Brae Oldest Tomb of Eagles Stalled cairns Ness of Brodgar earliest
c.3100	Quanterness Cairn *Grooved Ware* pottery Knap of Howar latest
c.3000	Wall of Brodgar built Standing Stones Quoyness Skara Brae phase II
c.2700	Ness of Brodgar 1, 8 & 12 Maeshowe built
c.2600	Ness of Brodgar 10 built Barnhouse 8 built Ring of Brodgar
c.2500	Ness of Brodgar 10 Latest chambered cairns
c.2300	Ness of Brodgar 10 infilled
c.2200	Latest Skara Brae dates
c.2100	Latest Ness of Brodgar
c.2000	Bronze Age burials

Ring of Brodgar - aerial view from the north-west

THE RING OF BRODGAR (ON *Bruar-gardr*, Bridge Farm) is situated on a peninsula between the Lochs of Harray and Stenness, in the heart of the West Mainland. This very fine stone circle originally comprised 60 megaliths, of which 27 remain upright. It is a perfect circle, 103.7m in diameter and is surrounded by a rock-cut ditch 10m across and over 3m deep.

Dating from the same Neolithic period as Maeshowe and Skara

Brae, the construction of the henge and ditch would have taken a lot of labour, implying an organised society with spare resources and some kind of strong beliefs. As with Maeshowe, the monument has been carefully situated, with clear views in all directions.

The monoliths resemble the uprights within Maeshowe in size and shape, ranging from about 2m to 4.5m in height, and often with angular faces or notches on

one side. They are all aligned with their flat sides facing into the centre of the circle.

There is an outlying standing stone, the Comet Stone, to the south east as well as several mounds nearby which could date from the Bronze Age. They may perhaps be points for viewing the variety of solar alignments relating to the solstices, equinoxes, Beltane and other dates which have been observed or suggested.

Ring of Brodgar - panoramic view from the centre of the ring - looking towards Harray Loch

This may have been the intention of the designer or not, but will always remain enigmatic. Alignments with lunar phenomena have also been observed and suggested, particularly at the times of major lunar standstills, every 18.6 years.

Nowhere does the feeling of space, where water, land and sky all seem to merge, feel stronger than at Brodgar. The constantly changing Orkney light and weather mean that the site can be visited at any season or time of day and always look different. Although we know little about the beliefs of the Neolithic people who built the Ring of Brodgar it is clear that they were a highly motivated and imaginative society.

Ring of Brodgar midsummer sunrise

Ring of Brodgar midsummer sunset

The Comet Stone

The Ring of Brodgar takes on a pristine appearance in the snow

The Ness of Brodgar

Ness of Brodgar under excavation

The Ness of Brodgar is the narrow peninsula north of the bridge from which the area takes its name. In 1925 a stone decorated with Neolithic lozenges and chevrons was found in the area now being excavated, having been reused as the lid of a Bronze Age cist burial.

Discovery The site was revealed by geophysical surveys in 2003. After exploratory digging in 2004, excavations have been carried out here annually ever since. So far only a small fraction of the buildings have been investigated.

Walls The site is bounded to the north and south by well built walls. The northern one was initially 4m wide, and up to 100m long. The walls were paved on the outside and must have been most impressive when built. Originally they could have been 3m or more high and enclosed an area roughly 125m by 75m. The oldest radiocarbon dates found so far are from material under the southern wall and are from c.3200-3100BC.

Buildings The largest building, structure 10, is 20m square with walls 5m thick. It is surrounded by paving and has stonework of remarkable quality. The cross shaped interior includes standing stones and in design is reminiscent of Maeshowe, with which the entrance seems to be aligned.

All of these buildings have side chambers built into the walls, central fireplaces and are aligned roughly north to south. Large quantities of *Grooved Ware* pottery and other artefacts have been found. In 2011 the *"Brodgar Boy"* clay figurine added to the growing finds of anthropomorphic artefacts in Orkney.

Painted Stones One of the most interesting finds was painted stones. Iron based pigment mixed with animal fat or egg whites were used to create the yellow, red and brown coatings. Some have scratched designs which resemble other incised Neolithic artwork.

Carved stone from the Ness

Broken mace head

Flagstone Roofs These buildings may have been partly roofed by flagstone slates in a similar manner to traditional Orkney houses. A layer of large, worked, rectangular flagstones was discovered on the floor of two of the structures. These well formed "slates" had been skillfully trimmed.

Interiors Dressers and central hearths similar to those at Skara Brae were present, but the scale of the buildings and lack of evidence for long term occupation suggests that these were not houses for living in. More probably they were used for special occasions as has also been suggested for those at Barnhouse Village.

Abandonment The latest radiocarbon dates so far found are c.2300BC from cattle bones round Structure 10. This was first built around 2600BC and involved much demolition and burial of earlier buildings. Development continued for about another 300 years, after which Structure 10 was put out of use. It was filled with midden and rubble.

Hundreds of cattle tibia were also found here, perhaps representing feasting at the final closure of the site. Neolithic cultural activity continued for perhaps another 200 years, but on a minor scale.

Nick Card, Project Manager, has said, *"The discoveries are unparalleled in British prehistory, the complexity of finds is changing the whole vision of what the landscape was 5,000 years ago and that it's of a scale that almost relates to the classical period in the Mediterranean with walled enclosures and precincts. The site could be more important than Stonehenge."*

Excavation work in progress 2008

Arrow head

Brodgar Stone found in 1925

High quality stonework and paved path

North Wall of Brodgar

Side cell

THE STANDING STONES OF STENNESS

Standing Stones of Stenness - midwinter sunset

THE STANDING STONES OF STENNESS originally comprised of a circle of perhaps 12 monoliths, surrounded by a ditch 2m deep, 7m wide and 44m in diameter. The tallest stone is over 5m high. In addition there is a hearth-like stone setting in the centre. The site dates from about 3000BC and is thus older than Maeshowe or Brodgar.

Socket holes for more stones or wooden uprights were also discovered within the circle and nearby, suggesting that the site was ori-

ginally more complex. The cove structure within the ring may have alignments with Maeshowe and Unstan Cairn.

The nearby Watchstone stands at the side of the Loch of Stenness. Observed from here some days before and after the winter solstice, the sun disappears behind the southern flank of the Ward Hill of Hoy, and then reappears momentarily on the north side, before finally setting.

There are several other stand-

ing stones in the vicinity, th Barnhouse Stone near the ma road, and a pair of smaller mon liths on the north side of t Brodgar Bridge. In addition the used to be the Stone of Odin.

This famous landmark was des crated and broken in 1814 to build a shed. It had a ho through which lovers and othe could hold hands and thus se their vows. The Oath of Od was binding on any contract, an also credited with healing power

Standing Stones of Stenness with the Hoy Hills and the Loch of Stenness

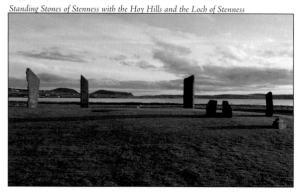

The Stone of Od

arnhouse Stone

Watchstone - midsummer sunset

ARNHOUSE VILLAGE Nearby the Neolithic Village of arnhouse on the edge of the och of Harray. The bases of at ast 15 free-standing houses are idicated here, each with a central earth, and beds similar to those : Skara Brae. Two were bigger an the rest, the largest being 7m quare internally with 3m thick alls. At midsummer the set-ng sun shines directly down the ntrance passage of one house.

hese structures resemble some of ie chambered cairns, especially Maeshowe. This may have been meeting-place associated with vents at the Standing Stones. lint and other stone tools were ound as well as Grooved Ware ottery, similar to that from Skara ›rae, the Standing Stones and the Jess of Brodgar.

There are strong similarities with the apparently slightly later struc-tures at the Ness of Brodgar, just over the bridge from here. Clearly much remains to be discovered about this fascinating area of Neolithic Orkney. This is all part of the enigmatic story of Orkney's archaeology.

Grooved Ware pottery

Hoy Hills and Loch of Stenness - midwinter sunset with "flashing" sun

arnhouse midsummer sunset

Barnhouse Neolithic village - large house entrance

Winter sunset down the passage on 12ᵗʰ January - www.maeshowe.co.uk

slabs which have been expertly c▮ and positioned. Also the moun▮ has been carefully situated wit▮ the entrance passage aligned suc▮ that the setting sun illuminate▮ the chamber for several weeks ▮ the afternoon before and after th▮ winter solstice.

Very few artefacts were foun▮ when the mound was cleare▮ out in 1862, but the discover▮ of a large number of 12ᵗʰ cer▮ tury Norse runic inscription▮ and other carvings somewh▮ mitigated this. These runes wer▮ carved about 1153 by Norseme▮ returning from the crusades an▮ are of the form "Ingibiorg, th▮ fair widow..." or "Thorfinn carve▮ these runes".

The chamber measures 4.5▮ square, similar to the smalle▮ houses at Skara Brae, while th▮ passage is 14.5m long and 1.4▮ high. It is lined with very larg▮ stone slabs, each of which weigh▮ several tons. The three chamber▮ are similarly roofed with sing▮ huge flagstones. The mound ▮ surrounded by a ditch datin▮ from about 2750BC, but the ban▮ seems to be more recent.

Maeshowe is very prominent i▮ the Stenness landscape. The qual▮ ity of its construction remair▮ supremely impressive 5,000 year▮ after it was built. It is high▮ doubtful whether the expertis▮ to quarry, transport and assem▮ ble these massive flagstones exist▮ today. Today's visitors can on▮ marvel at the abilities of thes▮ Neolithic builders and wonde▮ how they managed to do it all.

There are a number of othe▮ Maeshowe-type chambered cairr▮ to visit in Orkney including thos▮ at Cuween Hill near Finstowr▮ on Wideford Hill near Kirkwal▮ and at Quoyness in Sanday. Th▮ other type is referred to as th▮

MAESHOWE, or *Orkahaugr* in the *Orkneyinga Saga*, is one of the finest of all chambered cairns, of which there are many in Orkney. These tombs were built by Neolithic people from around 3200BC and were often used over a long period. Maeshowe dates from perhaps around 2700BC and is the largest and most splendid of its type to Orkney.

The stonework is engineered with great skill, with massive stone

"Ingibiorg" runes carved by 12ᵗʰ century Vikings

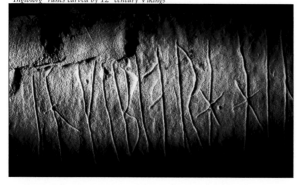

Orkney-Cromarty group, which have upright "stalls", shelves at one or both ends and corbelled roofs. They may also have cells leading off the main chamber at floor level. Examples include Unstan in Stenness, the Tomb of the Eagles in South Ronaldsay as well as several on Rousay.

Excavation of a few of these cairns has yielded the remains of large numbers of people, and provided much information on lifestyle, life expectancy and diseases suffered as well as artefacts such as pottery and tools. Two distinct types of the latter, *"Grooved Ware"* and *"Unstan Ware"*, have been found.

Some of the tombs seem to have been associated with a particular creature, such as Sea Eagles at the eponymous Tomb of the Eagles, and dogs at Cuween. The Neolithic people went to great lengths to provide "houses for the dead" and clearly their ancestors were very important to them. The cairns may well have been used for rituals as well as burials.

Whether Maeshowe was ever used as a tomb is unknown, but its ambience today is rather that of a "Neolithic Cathedral" than a burial chamber. Its solitary grandeur is perhaps being challenged by recent dramatic discoveries at the Ness of Brodgar.

Maeshowe from the northeast

Maeshowe sunset
Maeshowe sunset

Maeshowe interior showing passage, pillars and construction

Maeshowe aerial view from the south-west

The Maeshowe "dragon"

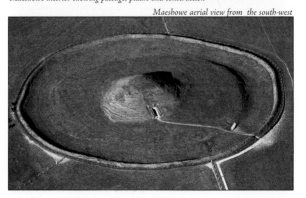

Orkney Peedie Guide 4th edition (r2) by Charles Tait

Marwick Head and Kitchener Memorial

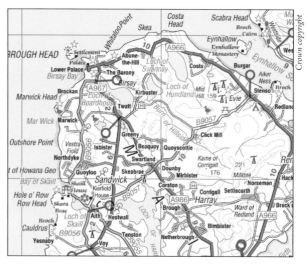

THE BROUGH OF BIRSAY

THE BROUGH OF BIRSAY is a tidal island off the northwest corner of the Mainland. There are remains of a large Viking settlement, which is underlain by Pictish buildings. Bronze casting was done here in Pictish times and a large symbol stone was also found. Settlement seems to have started about the 6th century AD.

Most of the ruins visible today are Viking, the small church is 12th century, but there may be an earlier Celtic one below it. On the slopes above the church are the outlines of several Norse longhouses up to 20m long, together with outhouses, which can be clearly seen from the air.

Near the church lies an extensive area of buildings, complete with bath-house and under floor central heating. It is thought that Earl Thorfinn the Mighty's 11th century cathedral and palace were in the village, which is called "The Palace".

On the Point of Buckquoy a number of figure-of-eight shaped Pictish houses of similar age to the one at Gurness have been excavated, but none are on display. "Groatie Buckies" (Cowrie Shells) may be found on the beach here in compensation.

Apart from the ancient monuments, the Brough has a light-house dating from 1925, and whole area is a very pleasant pl for a walk or to watch rough s from the shelter of the car dur a winter storm. It is also possi to see Puffins here during breeding season.

The Earl's Palace at "The Pala village was built by Earl Rob Stewart in the late 16th centu and consists of four wings su rounding a large courtyard whi has a well in the middle. It v said to be "a sumptuous and sta ly mansion" in 1633. Stewart w a half-brother of Mary Que of Scots.

The large exposed bay to the e of the Brough is called Skipi G There is a fine walk from the park to the Whale Bone, fro where there are spectacular vie on rough days. In summer whole area is awash with w flowers, including Thrift, Spr Squill, Grass of Parnassus a Sea Plantain.

To the south the Birsay Links a large area of sand dunes a machair. They are a sea of c our with wild flowers in summ There are fine views over Birs Bay from Garson, on the sou side. A path leads all the way Marwick Head from here.

Marwick Head (87m) lies abe 4km (2.5mi) to the south of T

Brough of Birsay from the south with a rough sea

...lica of Pictish Symbol Stone

100th anniversary of sinking of HMS Hampshire, at the Kitchener Memorial

Skipi Geo and the Whalebone on a midsummer evening

...lace. The tower at the highest ...int was erected after WW1 to ...mmemorate the Minister of ...ar, Kitchener, and the crew of ...MS Hampshire, which was sunk ...a German mine here in 1916. ...e cruiser was heading to Russia ...en the sinking happened. ...ere were very few survivors.

RSPB Bird Reserves Marwick Head is one of nearly twenty nature reserves in Orkney. In early summer it teems with breeding seabirds and is a very good place to view Guillemots, Razorbills, Fulmars, Kittiwakes, Rock Doves, Puffins, and even perhaps a Peregrine. The cliff-

...ough of Birsay aerial view showing Viking Age ruins

WEST MAINLAND

BIRSAY

Brough of Birsay
The Palace
Earl's Palace
Skipi Geo
Barony Water Mill
Marwick Head
Kirbuster Farm Museum

SANDWICK

Bay of Skaill
Skara Brae
Skaill House
Yesnaby

EVIE

Broch of Gurness
Aikerness Beach
Eynhallow Sound

HARRAY

Corrigall Farm Museum
Click Mill

STENNESS

Maeshowe
Standing Stones of Stenness
Ness of Brodgar
Barnhouse Settlement
Ring of Brodgar

ORPHIR

St Nicholas Round Kirk
Waulkmill Bay
Houton Viewpoint

Bay of Skaill & Yesnaby

Yesnaby Castle

The North Side, Bir

tops are carpeted by a profusion of Thrift, other wild flowers and yellow lichens in summer, which adds to the untamed wild beauty of the cliffs.

The Old Red Sandstone rock has level beds and weathers into a myriad of small ledges which are ideal for nesting seabirds. There are also plentiful food supplies in the neighbouring waters.

Other RSPB Reserves in the West Mainland include the Loons, near Marwick Head, the Birsay Moors, Cottascarth in Firth and Hobbister in Orphir. Other good places for birds are the Loch of Harray, Burgar Hill in Evie, the Loch of Skaill and Stromness Harbour.

Bay of Skaill Further south along the west coast of the Mainland lies the Bay of Skaill. The famous Neolithic village of Skara Brae is on the southwest shore. Skaill House is adjacent and shares ticketing with its more ancient

neighbour. A stroll here is much recommended at any season, whether benign on a summer's day or wild in a winter storm.

The Bow Head is on the south side of the bay and has superb views to north and south. The Hole o' Row is a natural arch, through which waves explode on a rough day. There is a superb cliff-top walk from the Bay of Skaill to Yesnaby, with its wild cliff scenery.

Yesnaby During a storm huge waves crash into and over the west coast cliffs. The Castle of Yesnaby is a mini version of the Old Man of Hoy, which can be seen from here. This coastal scenery is nature in the raw. Stromatolites, fossils which date from about 350 million years ago, may be seen here. There are also igneous dykes, granite intrusions and ancient lake beds to explore.

Yesnaby has many characters depending on the season, time of day and weather. On a gen-

tle summer's evening it appea benign and welcoming. During northwesterly force 12 gale wi enormous seas breaking, the r power of nature is laid bare.

Wild Flowers This exposed pla is one of the best places to s the rare endemic, *Primula scoti* It flowers in May and July a can be spotted from the approa road. This hardy little plant o grows in Orkney and the nor coast of Scotland. It has sm magenta flowers. In summ Spring Squill, Thrift, Grass Parnassus and Sea Plantain gi the maritime heath a warm glov

The North Side From The Pala the road returns to Kirkwall cloc wise via Evie and Rendall. Cos Head above the Loch of Swann was the site of early aerogenerat experiments. Today Burgar H and nearby Hammars Hill a home to some of the hundreds wind turbines which are now common in Orkney.

Primula scotica

Grass of Parnassus

Spring Squill

Skaill House from the west

SKAILL HOUSE is situated near Skara Brae on the west coast of the Mainland. It is the only mansion house in Orkney open to the public as a museum and dates partly from the 17th century, when part of the Earldom estate passed to the Bishopric under Bishop Graham in 1615.

This Bishop "acquired" a substantial amount of land from bishopric property and smallholdings, in the name of his eldest son, John, who became the first Laird. The present Laird, Major Malcolm Macrae, is the 12th. The property is now a very interesting visitor

attraction, jointly ticketed with nearby Skara Brae.

The oldest part was built by Bishop Graham in the 1620's. Much of the house dates from the 18th century, with further additions over the next two centuries.

The tour is an insight to the lives of the Lairds and their families, with connections to many historic events. These include some of Captain Cook's dinner service, a cupboard called the Armada Chest, with panels said to have come from a Spanish ship in 1588 and one of Bishop Graham's beds.

The house is allegedly haunted, and during renovation work 15 skeletons were found near the east porch, which are thought to be early Christian, perhaps Pictish.

There is a gift shop and the property is open from April to October. A visit makes an interesting contrast to Skara Brae.

Other mansion houses which may be visited include Balfour Castle on Shapinsay, Carrick House on Eday and Melsetter House on Hoy, all by arrangement.

Dining Room

Bishop Graham's bed

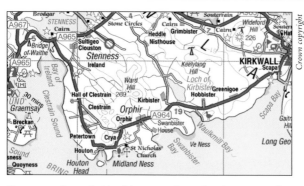

Orphir Round Chu

ORPHIR, on the south side of the West Mainland, faces the wide expanse of Scapa Flow. There are excellent viewpoints along the A964 at Greenigoe, Hobbister, Houton and Scorradale. From the summit of the Ward Hill (268m) a 360° panorama unfolds, taking in all of the West Mainland, Hoy, Scapa Flow and Scotland in the distance.

Waulkmill Bay is a wide sheltered and shallow sandy inlet, ideal for seaside fun with the family. This is one of the best places for bathing in Orkney as the sun heats

up the sand and water on a fine summer's day.

St Nicholas Round Kirk was built by Earl Haakon c.1123 in atonement for the death of St Magnus. Only the apse survives of this little gem of a building. The Earl's Bu is mentioned numerous times in the *Orkneyinga Saga* and may well have been situated here. The nearby Orkneyinga Saga Centre provides interpretation.

Houton is now the ferry terminal for Lyness and Flotta. During WWI there was a large flying

boat base here. In Novemb 1918 the German High Se Fleet was interned in Scapa Flc before being scuttled in Ju 1919. The famous photograp by Tom Kent were taken fr here. Perhaps Houton Head the best vantage point. There a remains of a coast battery a signal station here, used in WV and WWII. The gun hous searchlight enclosures and oth buildings can be explored.

The Hall of Clestrain overloo the Bring Deeps and Hoy H This was the birthplace of John Rae the famous 19th ce tury Arctic explorer whose stc is told in the Stromness Museu Though now derelict there a plans for its restoration.

Unstan Cairn is off the A965 ne the Brig o' Waithe in Stenne This Neolithic chambered ca is a hybrid with both stalls and side cell. In contrast to Maesho this site is always freely open a never crowded.

Panoramic View from the Summit of the Ward Hill

Waulkmill Bay

Unstan Ca

FARM MUSEUMS & MILLS

FARM MUSEUMS Kirbuster in Birsay and Corrigall in Harray, are in strong contrast to Skaill House and represent examples of ordinary houses from the early and late 19th century respectively. Both have a dwelling house, byre, barn, corn drying kiln and outhouses.

Kirbuster Farm has no chimney, but instead an open fire with a "fireback" and a wooden smokehole in the roof with "skylin". The smoke-hole also served to let extra light in. There is a neuk bed, reminiscent of the beds at Skara Brae built into one wall. Despite the lack of a chimney the house is not very smoky inside.

Corrigall Farm is more modern with chimneys and a higher roof but is otherwise similar. The bedroom end has boxbeds, and the floors are all of flagstone. On display are a variety of old implements, traditional crafts, furnishings and tools, as well as a variety of livestock.

The Click Mill near Dounby is a late 19th century example of a so-called "Norse" vertical axis corn mill. Named because of the noise made during operation, these were basically mechanised quernstones. They were common from Norse, or earlier times, until the later 19th century when larger water mills became popular.

Barony Mill is a restored 19th century watermill powered by water from the nearby Loch of Boardhouse. Built in 1873, it still grinds grain in the winter. It incorporates a kiln for drying the corn at the east end and mostly produces beremeal from old fashioned 6 row Bere Barley. The 4.1m overshot wheel turns at 12rpm and is said to use about half a million litres of water per hour under full load.

Kirbuster Museum showing fireback

Corrigall Farm Museum

Click Mill

Boardhouse Mill

THE BROCH OF GURNESS, EVIE

The Broch of Gurness with surrounding settlement, ditches and ramparts

BROCHS (ON *Borg*, stronghold) are unique to Scotland and Orkney has about 100. They developed from roundhouses which first appeared around 700BC. Brochs typically have a large tower, up to 20m in diameter with hollow walls up to 5m thick at the base.

The walls have an internal staircase and the structures could be up to 15m tall. Most brochs are on or near the coast, but several in the West Mainland are sited inland. Most are solitary; some are surrounded by settlements.

Broch of Gurness Over 2,000 years after its construction, this

broch at Aikerness remains imposing. The site, with its ramparts, ditches, broch tower and extensive surrounding settlement, is an evocative place to visit. It was occupied from the Iron Age through Pictish to Norse times.

The broch is surrounded by three massive ramparts and deep ditches, and may well have had a tall tower. Inside there is a central hearth and an elaborate underground well with a collecting tank. The space between the broch and the defences encloses a small village which could have been occupied by 30 or so families. An imposing entrance leads via a small street to the broch

doorway with its massive lintel.

The houses share walls and a furnished in stone with hearth cooking tanks, drains, box bec storage cupboards and even to lets. Unlike at other monument the visitor is free to wander at w and imagine life millenia ago.

During excavation many artefac were found, including fragmen of Roman amphorae from abou 100AD, stone and bone too pottery and items with Pictis Ogam inscriptions. A 9th centu Viking female burial comple with grave goods was present ne the top of the mound.

The Broch of Gurness from the entrance on the east side

The Broch of Gurness from the west with surrounding ditches and ramparts

ikerness Beach (or the Sands f Evie) faces Eynhallow Sound nd Rousay. This attractive beach backed by a large area of sand unes. Seals, Otters and seaducks nay be seen round the shores. he dunes, shoreline and banks f the burn are all good places for ild flowers.

Pictish Houses A group of hamrock-shaped multicellu-r Pictish houses stands at the ntrance to the Broch of Gurness. hey are the only examples cur-ently on view in Orkney and ere rebuilt here after the excav-ions. Originally they stood on ne broch mound. The museum as a shop, and interpretation.

Other Brochs Other excavated brochs include Midhowe on Rousay, Burgar in Sandwick, Burrian on North Ronaldsay and Burroughstone on Shapinsay. Many more are visible as mounds throughout Orkney, even inland in Harray.

Earthhouses Another interesting development starting in c.600BC is the Earthhouse or souterrain. Examples at Rennibister in Firth and Grain near Kirkwall can be visited. These underground structures may be cellars from long-gone roundhouses. They probably used for storage, and any resemblance to chambered cairns is most likely superficial.

Orkney Museum

Pictish comb

Orkney Museum

Pictish symbol from Broch of Gurness

ictish houses at Gurness

Rennibister Earthhouse

STROMNESS

Stromness from the fer

STROMNESS (ON *Straum-nes, Stream Point*) was also called *Hamnavoe* (Harbour Bay) by the Vikings. This excellent harbour is the ferry terminal for the crossing to Scrabster in Caithness. There are also many small fishing boats and dive boats which work from here. One of Orkney's three RNLI Lifeboats is based here.

The town dates from the 17th century and for many years supplied water, stores and crewmen to vessels taking the northern route around Britain as well as ships of the Hudson's Bay Company and whalers. During the Herring Boom in the late 19th and early 20th centuries it was also very busy.

Street The winding, flagstone-paved street is the backbone of the town. Many of the houses on the shore side have their own

piers, while the upslope houses are reached by a multitude of narrow lanes. Lack of space for new development has ensured that the town has retained its attractive character, with the industrial area on the outskirts.

The intimate nature of the town makes Stromness popular with visitors and several events take place here including the Orkney Traditional Folk Festival, the Stromness Shopping Week and a Beer Festival.

Museum Stromness Museum has a fascinating series of displays on mostly maritime and natural history themes. These include the Hudson's Bay Company connection, and the scuttle of the WW1 German High Seas Fleet. There are also extensive exhibits of Orkney birds, mammals, molluscs and insects.

John Rae was born at the Hall Clestrain in 1813. He had a lor career as a doctor and surveyo with the Hudson's Bay Compar in northern Canada. He is be remembered for discoverin the fate of the 1845 Frankli Expedition to the Arctic.

Rae was the foremost 19th cer tury expert in Arctic travel ar survival. The Stromness Museur has many artefacts related to hir including an innovative inflatabl boat and his violin. There is memorial to him in St Magnu Cathedral.

Pier Arts Centre Also an esser tial visit, the Pier Arts Centre ha a permanent collection of 20th century art and holds regular tem porary exhibitions. This attrac ive old building was once th agency and store for the Hudson Bay Company and is built on

Pier Arts Centre

Stromness - Victoria Stre

Hoy Sound and the Hoy Hills from Outertown

...ier near the ferry terminal. It ...as recently been refurbished and ...xtended to accommodate a great-...r variety of work.

Shopping There are many inter-...sting shops in Stromness, offer-...ng a range of local crafts, knit-...ear, books and art, as well as sev-...ral grocers and hardware shops. ...arking is not very practical in the ...arrow street but there are plenty ...f spaces on the approach road.

Ness Coast Gun Battery was an ...mportant part of the defence of ...capa Flow in both World Wars. ...he WWII structures are largely ...ntact and include 6in gun hous-...s, the battery observation post, ...nagazines, generator houses and ...ervice accommodation.

Activities Apart from the time-...ess attraction of watching boats ...nd people around the harbour,

Stromness has a golf course and a variety of fine walks. There is an excellent panoramic view from Brinkie's Brae (94m) above the town.

Warebeth beach lies to the west and offers fine views of the Hoy Hills and Hoy Sound. There is a fine coastal walk to it via the Point of Ness, which continues westwards to Breckness. This shore has many interesting rock formations which date from 350 million years ago.

Black Craig At the north end of Outertown, the Black Craig (111m) offers a fine panorama from the old coastguard hut. A little further on is North Gaulton Castle, a fine, but little visited, rock stack. At Billia Cru the European Marine Energy Centre has testbeds for wave energy devices which may be visible.

John Rae

Stromness has narrow winding streets

Ness Gun Battery dates from WWI and WWII

STROMNESS

Hamnavoe (Harbour)
Pier Arts Centre
Stromness Museum
The Street
Login's Well
The Cannon
Point of Ness
Ness Gun Battery
EMEC Test Centre
Warebeth Beach
Black Craig

Holm Sound and the Churchill Barriers from the north

German High Seas Fleet in Scapa Flow, November 1919

SCAPA FLOW was used as the main base of the British Home Fleet in both WW1 and WWII due to it being a large land-locked harbour with deep entrances and deep water anchorages. In both wars it took some time to make it secure.

WWI Early in the First World War, Scapa Flow was selected as the main base for the British Home Fleet. In 1914 it had no defences in place, but by 1918 it was very heavily defended. Coastal batteries, boom defence nets, controlled minefields and many other measures were put in place to make the fleet safe in its anchorage. Early experiments with shipborne aircraft were carried out here for the first time.

Scuttle of German Fleet Th harbour saw dramatic actions i both wars. After WW1, 74 ve sels of the German High Se Fleet were interned here, and c 21st June 1919 they were scuttle Some were beached, but mo sank. The majority were salvage during the 1920s and 1930s, b three battleships and four cruiser remain and are much visited b scuba divers today.

WWII At the start of the Secon World War, Scapa Flow had a fe gun emplacements left over fro the previous conflict. It was soc realised that extensive defence would be required to render Scap Flow secure from German attack

HMS *Royal Oak* In 1939 th German U-boat *U47* crept int Scapa Flow through Holm Soun and torpedoed HMS *Royal Oa* with the loss of 833 crew. Th resulted in the construction c the Churchill Barriers and a hug increase in the defences in genera

The wreck of HMS *Royal Oa* was leaking considerable quan tities of fuel oil and became pollution threat. As a result th Royal Navy has removed much c the oil fuel that remained aboard

"SMS Bayern" sinking in 1919 in Scapa Flow

Diver examines gun on WW2 German wreck "SMS Dresden"

Churchill Barriers Greatly increased defences were ordered to be built by Churchill in 1940 after the sinking of HMS *Royal Oak* to seal off the eastern approaches to Scapa Flow. The firm of Balfour Beatty was appointed as contractors. To solve the labour shortage, several hundred Italian prisoners of war were drafted in from Libya early in 1942 to assist in the work.

Camps and works were set up in the East Mainland as well as on Lamb Holm, Glimps Holm and Burray. Nearly 1 million cubic metres of rock in wire bolsters was used to complete the four barriers, and by late 1942 they were breaking the surface. Over 60,000 5 and 10-ton concrete blocks were used to clad the sides.

WWII Defences Up to 40,000 men were based in Orkney at the peak of activity in WWII. Once secured, maximum advantage was taken of the strategically important position of Scapa Flow. Much evidence still remains of the defences, including coastal batteries, searchlight emplacements, old airfields, and parts of the naval base at Lyness on Hoy.

During WWII, aircraft carriers were very important and Orkney served as a base for repairs and training for many of their aircraft.

"HMS Royal Oak" firing her main armament

Blockships before Barrier No 3 was built

Barriers Nos 1, 2 and 3 with blockships in WWII

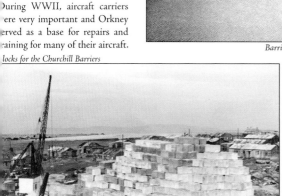
Blocks for the Churchill Barriers

SCAPA FLOW

Ness Gun Battery
Stromness Museum
Houton
WWI German Fleet
Hatston Industrial Estate
Kirkwall Airport
Netherbutton Radar Station
Churchill Barriers
Italian Chapel
Hoxa Head Batteries
Lyness Naval Base
Scapa Flow Visitor Centre
Hackness Martello Tower
Flotta Oil Terminal

SCAPA FLOW

Coastal Defence Battery overlooking Holm Sound

"Swordfish" aircraft at Hatston Airfield, "HMS Sparrowhawk"

Aircraft Carrier "HMS Victorious"

Scapa Flow panoramic view from Glimps Holm

The action where Bismarck wa sunk succeeded due to the seem ingly archaic Fairey Swordfis torpedo bombers which dogged searched out the battleship and despite their apparent frailt damaged the ship's rudder.

Scapa Flow Visitor Centre, base in the old pumphouse at Lynes is a museum and interpretatio centre about the wartime histor of Scapa Flow. Lyness was major naval base in both Worl Wars. During WWII large o tanks were built into Wee Fe the hill above the harbour. Man artefacts are on display from bot wars, ranging from large guns t small items. The remaining larg oil tank is also used for exhibits.

North Sea Oil In the 1970s c was first exploited in the Nort Sea, and the Flotta Oil Termin continues to process and expo large quantities of crude. Tanke remain a common sight in Scap Flow. In addition, vessels doir ship to ship transfers or unde going maintenance often call.

Wildlife Scapa Flow is winte home to many birds which bree in the Arctic, including Grea Northern Divers and Long-taile Ducks. The Churchill Barrier are a good place to look for thes species. In summer many Tern Eiders, Red-breasted Merganser and other seabirds nest aroun the shores.

t is occasionally visited by pods of young Sperm Whales and various species of dolphins, including Killer Whales and Porpoises. The shores are home to the elusive Otter, while Common and Grey Seals both breed in the area.

Transport Link The Barriers provide Orkney's only fixed transport links between the Mainland and other islands. Large sandy beaches have built up in Weddel and Water Sound on the east sides of Barriers No 3 and No 4. The blockage of the channels has also greatly affected the distribution of sand all around Orkney.

Weather The Barriers are subject to adverse weather conditions. Storm waves can make crossing dangerous, particularly at high spring tides. Most visitors, however, will only see Scapa Flow in beautiful, benign and colourful summer weather.

Scapa Flow Visitor Centre Pump House

Gun mounted on Hackness Martello Tower at Longhope on Hoy

Oil Tanker in Scapa Flow

Twin 6-pounder gun crew

Flotta Oil Terminal

The Aurora Borealis is often seen during the winter in Orkney

EAST MAINLAND

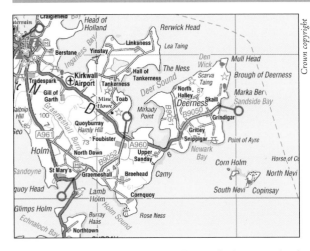

EAST MAINLAND The parishes of Tankerness, Holm and Deerness have much to offer, having a charm all of their own, like a separate island in many ways. The area is generally low lying and mostly farmland, but all the same has much of interest to see and do. This includes many fine beaches, some spectacular cliffs and good walking.

Archaeology There is ample evidence of early occupation in the form of burnt mounds and brochs, most notably Dingieshowe on the Deerness isthmus. Minehowe is an enigmatic, well-like Iron Age structure. It has 29 stone steps which descend in two flights to a small chamber. Minehowe is a small part of a large unexplored prehistoric landscape, but is not currently open to the public.

Rerwick Head is the most north-easterly point of Tankerness. In both World Wars there were gun batteries on this headland, which may still be seen. There are fine coastal walks from here, southwards along the low cliffs to the Ness and Hall of Tankerness, or eastwards to the fine beaches at Heatherhouse and Redbanks.

Mull Head in Deerness is a Nature Reserve with indicated paths. Near the entrance the Gloup is a large partially collapsed cave, a deep chasm which can be observed with care from a gallery.

The low cliffs at Mull Head are a good place to see seabirds and seals. There is a fine circular walk around the headland.

Brough of Deerness On the east side of Mull Head , about 1km north of the carpark, stands the promontory of the Brough of Deerness. There is a small chapel and a scatter of foundations of buildings. All are Norse, but Pictish people were probably here in earlier times.

Covenanters' Memorial This tower on the north side of Deerness is a poignant reminder of the spot where about 200 political prisoners were drowned in 1679. Over 1,200 Covenanters had been captured at the Battle of Bothwell Brig and held at Greyfriar's Kirkyard in Edinburgh. Those who were not executed or did not submit or die from exposure, were to be transported to the West Indies as slaves.

The *"Crown of London"* left Edinburgh in December 1679 The ship took shelter off Deerness but was driven ashore. The crew were saved, but only 50 of the prisoners survived. Most were soon caught and sent onwards to Jamaica. The Covenanters were vehemently opposed to the imposition of the Book of Common Prayer by Charles I and later Charles II.

Copinsay is a small island and RSPB Reserve off the southeast of Deerness. It has a large seabird colony in summer on its east facing cliffs. Many Grey Seals also pup here in autumn. It is hard to reach, but well worth the effort if a boat can be procured.

Holm The pretty village of St Mary's in Holm overlooks Holm Sound, through which U47 sailed

Rerwick Head September sunset

in 1939 on its way to sink HMS *Royal Oak*. There is a good view of the sound and the Churchill Barriers from the hill east of the village.

The fertile area in the south east corner is known as Paplay, where the Vikings found a large monastic settlement. No archaeological remains have been excavated from this time here, but a high status Pictish farmstead at Skaill in Deerness was examined some time ago.

Beaches In Deerness, Sandside, Newark and Dingieshowe are all very fine beaches for a walk or picnic. Keep a good look out at Newark Bay in case you should see the mermaid! There are several attractive small beaches in Tankerness. In Holm, Wester Sand and Howes Wick, near the Old Kirk, are pleasant.

Wildlife There are many good birding sites here including the flat muddy shores at Mill Sands and St Peter's Pool, in Tankerness. Lochs include St Mary's and Graemeshall in Holm, and the Loch of Tankerness. In Deerness Mull Head is home to breeding seabirds and moorland species. Tankerness is especially attractive to Short-eared Owls, especially while breeding.

Mull Head, Deerness from seaward

Covenanters' Memorial

Copinsay cliffs from the east

Newark Bay, where mermaids are said to appear

EAST MAINLAND

Rerwick Head
Minehowe
St Peter's Pool
Dingieshowe
Newark Bay
Sandside
The Gloup
Brough of Deerness
Mull Head
Covenanters' Memorial
Copinsay
St Mary's
Paplay
Holm Sound

Italian Chapel and Churchill Barriers

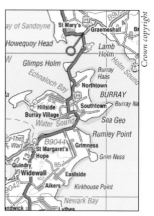

Crown copyright

The Italian Chapel was built by Italian prisoners of war in WWII

ITALIAN CHAPEL *"The Miracle of Camp 60"* was built by Italian prisoners of war of Camp 60, who arrived from Libya in January 1942 to help build the Churchill Barriers. It is an unusual survivor and memorial to the Second World War.

To brighten up the cheerless camp of Nissen huts the Italians made paths and planted flowerbeds. Artist, Domenico Chiocchetti made the St George and the Dragon statue from barbed wire and cement, to preside over the camp square. The prisoners soon had a theatre and a recreational hut complete with a concrete billiard table, but they lacked a chapel.

In late 1943 two Nissen huts were joined end to end and Chiocchetti set to work, aided by a small number of other POWs. One end was to be the Chapel, the other a school. The hut was lined with plasterboard and an altar with the rail cast in concrete.

Chiocchetti painted the Madonna and Child behind the altar. The image is based on a 19th century painting by Nicolo Barabino from a card his mother had given to him when he left for the war. He also frescoed a White Dove, the symbol of the Holy Spirit, at the centre of the vault and included the symbols of the four Evangelists around it, as well as two Cherubim and two Seraphim lower down.

The upper parts of the interio appear like brick with vaultin, while the lower walls are painte to resemble carved marble. Th "vaults" in the ceiling are espe cially well executed with quit stunning visual effect. Palumb a metalworker, made candleabr the rood screen and gates. Th façade was erected with the hel of Bruttapasta, with an archwa and pillars.

A belfry was mounted on to and a moulded head of Christ i red clay was placed on the fron of the arch. The whole exteric of the hut was then covered wit a thick coat of cement, never i short supply during the buildin of the Barriers!

The Chapel in 1944

The Italian Chapel with some of the Italian prisoners of w

The Italian Chapel interior

Chiocchetti returned to Orkney in 1960, when he did much to restore the internal paintwork of the chapel. In 1961 his hometown, Moena, near Bolzano in the Dolomites, gifted a wayside shrine, the carved figure of Christ erected outside the Chapel, to the people of Orkney. More recently much work has been done to restore and preserve the Chapel, the memorial statue and surroundings for the future.

The Italian Chapel is now one of the most visited monuments in Orkney and is a fitting memorial to those lost in wartime. Chiocchetti, in addressing the Orcadian people, said, "The chapel is yours, for you to love and preserve. I take with me to Italy the remem-

D Chiocchetti at work

brance of your kindness and wonderful hospitality. I shall remember you always, and my children shall learn from me to love you. I thank (you)....for having given me the joy of seeing again the little chapel of Lamb Holm where I, in leaving, leave a part of my heart."

It is somewhat ironic that most of the many visitors to Orkney

Head of Christ above the door

cross the Churchill Barriers to see the Chapel. They come not to remember the British war leader, or to marvel at military engineering, but to visit our little Italian shrine, which is a monument to hope and faith in exile. It is now 70 years ago that the prisoners from the Libyan desert arrived on a chilly Lamb Holm, but their chapel offers a warm welcome.

Antonella Papa at work in 2015

The Italian Chapel

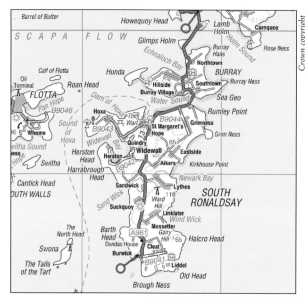

Crown copyright

(Bay), and not the English wor "hope". In the village are the O. Smiddy Museum, several inte esting shops and craft worksho as well as the Creel Restaurant.

Boys' Ploughing Match At Sar o' Wright, the Boys' Ploughin Match is held each August. Th girls dress up as horses and th boys as ploughmen, before bein judged as at a real horse even Later, rigs are worked in the sar using ploughs which have ofte been handed down over gener tions. Old timers then decide c the champion of the day.

Marine Life Aquarium Po Farmhouse "offers a uniqu chance to see and understan some aspects of the marir environment."

SOUTH RONALDSAY AND BURRAY are easily accessed from the Mainland by the Churchill Barriers. There are many sites of interest apart from the Barriers themselves, their associated blockships and the lovely sandy beaches which have built up at on the east side of No 3 and No 4.

Burray (ON *Borgarey*, Broch Island) is low lying with very fine beaches on the east side. Echnaloch is particularly good for wildfowl at all times of year. Many overwintering bird species can also be seen from the Barriers.

Orkney Fossil and Heritage Centre has displays of Orkney rocks and fossils and tells the story of Orkney's geology, as well as relics of bye-gone days. There is a gift shop and tea room, which is open from April to October.

South Ronaldsay (ON *Rognvald's-ey*, Rognvald's Island) has a special charm. The small village of St Margaret's Hope dates from the 17th and 18th centuries. The bay is said to be named after a 13th century Norse princess who died in 1290 while on her way to marry Prince Edward of England, but "Hope" comes from ON *Hjop*

Hoxa Tapestry Gallery Her Leila Thomson weaves wonderfi tapestries "inspired by the life an landscape of Orkney." Some her tapestries are on display her The shop sells framed prints and range of tapestry rugs.

The Tomb of the Eagles is t the south, near Burwick. Th Orkney-Cromarty type cham bered cairn is only one of tw which have been excavate recently, and strongly resemble Unstan Cairn in Stenness. Th remains of about 340 individua were found. Of particular inte

Fossil and Vintage Centre, Viewforth, Burray

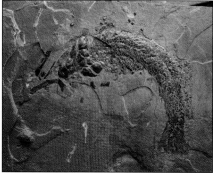

Boys' Ploughing Match, South Ronaldsay

st was the discovery of skeletons and talons of Sea Eagles - hence the name.

The cairn was built about 3150BC and used for up to 800 years. Over 40 broken *Unstan Ware* pots were found, as well as fish and animal bones and charred barley. Beautifully carved stone objects and rougher stone tools are on display along with some of the skulls in the museum where they can be examined closely. The human remains have revealed much about the people's lives.

Tomb of the Eagles, interior of the main chamber

The nearby Liddle Burnt Mound dates from the Bronze Age, from perhaps 1000BC. It has a central trough which was used to cook joints of meat by throwing in stones heated in a fire - hence the mound of burnt stones.

The Tomb of the Otters, near Skerries Bistro was discovered in 2010. This chambered cairn has five branches. Human remains dating from c.3000BC were found inside.

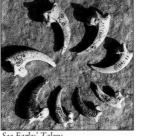
Sea Eagles' Talons

Skull from Tomb of the Eagles

Ferries John o' Groats Ferries runs in the summer between Caithness and Burwick in around 45 minutes. Pentland Ferries operates a daily roro catamaran ferry between Gills Bay and St. Margarets Hope, offering a scenic alternative to the route between Stromness and Scrabster.

The Bay of Cletts and St Peter's Kirk, East Side

St Margaret's Hope, South Ronaldsay

SOUTH RONALDSAY

Burray
Glimps Holm beaches
Fossil & Vintage Centre
4th Barrier beaches
St Margaret's Hope
Old Smiddy Museum
Hoxa Tapestry Centre
Boys' Ploughing Match
Newark Bay
Tomb of the Eagles

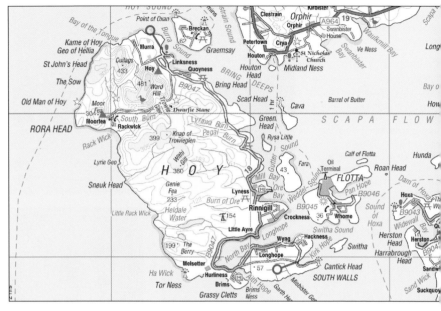

Hoy (ON *Ha-ey*, High Island) is the second largest of the Orkney Islands and different in character from the others. The north end is hilly with the Ward Hill (479m) and Cuilags (433m) being prominent landmarks from many parts of Orkney. Much of the north end of Hoy is an RSPB Reserve.

Old Man of Hoy The north and west coasts have spectacular cliffs, only the south end being low and fertile. One of Orkney's most well-known icons is the famous rock stack, the Old Man of Hoy (137m), which stands on a lava platform. The ferry passes the Hoy cliffs on its way across the Pentland Firth, allowing a stunning view of the noble stack.

Rackwick The wide sweep of Rackwick, on the north west side with a sand and boulder beach bounded on both sides by high cliffs, is well appreciated from the path to the Old Man. This offers good views across the Pentland Firth to Scotland. Rackwick has a beauty and climate all of its own, beware the midges but admire the dragonflies and wild flowers.

St John's Head The imposin craigs at St John's Head (351m are the highest vertical sea clif in Britain. The horizontal beds c sandstone have weathered to giv dramatic reds and yellows, whic are especially vibrant with a lo evening sun.

Dwarfie Stone Below the War Hill, on the road to Rackwick, lie the enigmatic Dwarfie Stone wit its hand carved chamber. Thi may be Neolithic, but is unique a the only such tomb in the UK. I must have taken a lot of work t excavate the cavity.

St John's Head (351m), Britain's highest vertical sea cliff, is one of "National Geographic's" top ten world ocean views

capa Flow There are good views cross Scapa Flow from the east past road to North and South Valls (ON Vagr, Voe or Bay). Most of the population lives at the south end, where the landscape is more like the rest of Orkney.

Vater of Hoy Near this small ch, a small, fenced memorial to etty Corrigall lies on the parish oundary. This young girl sadly ommitted suicide in the 19th ntury. She had become pregnant to a local man who subsequently left on a whaling ship for the Nor'West. She could not be uried in consecrated ground.

egal Burn, further south, is the rgest stream in Orkney. This ttractive watercourse and estuary a fine place for a picnic and also see an Otter if you are lucky. he shoreline has fabulously roded sandstone boulders.

yness was a large naval base uring both World Wars and as known as HMS Prosperine. Underground oil storage tanks, large harbour, dubbed "Golden Wharf" on account of its cost, and huge array of buildings sprang p. Most of the military detritus as been cleared up, and Lyness is ow the ferry terminal for Houton n the Mainland and for Flotta. he wharf area has now been conerted into harbour facilities, hard anding and warehouses.

Winter sunset from Rackwick beach at low tide

Lyness Naval Cemetery is a poignant reminder of the human sacrifice involved in wartime. There are memorials to British and German servicemen of both World Wars. These include some of those lost on HMS *Vanguard* which blew up in 1917 near Flotta and HMS *Royal Oak*, torpedoed in 1939. Recently, standing stones were erected near the ferry terminal remembering those lost in the WWII Russian convoys.

Russian Convoys Memorial

Dwarfie Stone

Hoy

Old Man of Hoy
Ward Hill
Rackwick
Dwarfie Stone
Pegal Burn & Water of Hoy
Lyness Naval Base
Scapa Flow Visitor Centre
Melsetter House
Longhope Lifeboat Museum
Hackness Martello Tower
Cantick Head lighthouse

Scapa Flow Visitor Centre

Wee Fea The Naval HQ and Communications Centre on Moor Fea, the hill above Lyness, has fine views over Scapa Flow and to the south. The hill here is honeycombed by giant underground tanks installed in WWII by Norwegian miners. A road

Longhope Lifeboat Memorial

Longhope Harbour

goes up to a wonderful viewpoint on Wee Fea.

Scapa Flow Visitor Centre is in what was the pumphouse serving the Royal Navy fuel oil tanks during WWII. One of the oil tanks has also been retained and contains displays of military equipment and artefacts. Inside the pumphouse the machinery has been renovated and there are displays of small artefacts, photographs and documents relating to the two World Wars. Outside several WWI German guns, railway stock used in WWII and a propeller off *HMS Hampshire* can be seen.

Melsetter House and Rysa Lodge were designed by William Lethaby in Arts and Crafts style for the Middlemore family. At Melsetter the original house dat-

ing from 1738 is part of the 189 design, forming the most attrac ive country house in Orkney. can be visited by arrangement.

Longhope Lifeboat Museum Brims is a museum whose ma exhibit is the lifeboat, Thom McCunn, which served here fro 1933 to 1962. Since being estal lished in 1874, many successf rescues were undertaken fro here. Perhaps the late coxswa Dan Kirkpatrick was the mc deserving of fame.

It was from here that he and h crew left in the lifeboat *TG* to go to the aid of a Liberia freighter, *Irene*, in March 196 Sadly all were lost in tumultt ous seas in the Pentland Firt A bronze statue in Osmondwa Cemetery honours the *TGB* cre The present Longhope Lifebo: The *Helen Comrie*, is of the late *Tamar* class, and was on station October 2006. She is based in t little harbour at Longhope.

Martello Tower & Battery *A* Hackness there is a Martel Tower and gun battery, one of tv in Scotland. It was built duri the early 19th century Napoleor Wars to protect shipping fro marauding American privatee Convoys were introduced at th time to guard merchant vesse from attack, and Longhope was good place for ships to gather.

The tower originally had 24-pounder gun mounted on to while the nearby battery had eig similar guns, with barracks, stor and a magazine. The site is no managed by Historic Scotlan and has been extensively renov: ed inside and out.

Cantick Head Lighthouse w completed in 1858 by Dav Stevenson and automated 1991. There are good views ov the Pentland Firth from her

Lyness from Wee Fea

iller Whales have been seen
ose in to the rocks here at times.

ature In contrast to the dra-
atic cliffs of North Hoy, the low
iffs, fine beaches and fertile land
ake for more gentle walking.
rimula scotica and other maritime
eath plants grow along the south
past. Otters and seals live around
e shores and many of Orkney's
haracteristic birds thrive here. In
inter North Bay is excellent for
aders and wintering wildfowl. A
ock of Barnacle Geese stays here
ch winter.

iking Drama Perhaps the most
teresting association dates from
95, when King Olaf Tryggvason
f Norway forcibly converted Earl
gurd the Stout to Christianity.
Osmondwall. Refusal meant
at the King would order the

death of Sigurd's son, so he chose
to accept. He subsequently
returned to his former ways and
died carrying the Raven Banner
at the Battle of Clontarf in 1014.
Sailing ships used the bay to wait
for the tide to turn or to shelter.

Transport Hoy can be reached by
the ferry MV *Hoy Head* which
runs from Houton in Orphir to
Lyness and Flotta. A passenger
ferry also runs from Stromness
to Moaness and Graemsay.
Accommodation, taxis, tours and
meals are available on the island.
The only shop is at Longhope.

Hackness Martello Tower

Melsetter House and Farm

Cantick Head Lighthouse

MV Hamnavoe in Hoy Sound with Graemesay and the Hoy Hills behind

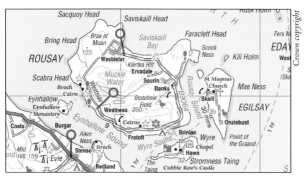

Westness Irish style broo

Rousay (ON *Hrolfs-ey*, Rolf's Island) has been called *"The Egypt of the North"* due to its concentration of prehistoric monuments. This round, hilly island has a road around the coast and makes a pleasant excursion from the Mainland via the roro ferry from Tingwall in Rendall.

Chambered Cairns Near the pier is the unusual two tiered chambered cairn of Taversoe Tuick. This unique little tomb also has two entrances. Further west are two more chambered cairns at Blackhammar and Yarso. Both are of the "stalled" type, divided up by upright slabs as in a byre.

Blackhammar contained only two burials and a broken Unstan Ware bowl, while Yarso had remains of at least 21 people. In both cases flint and bone tools were found as well as deer bones at Yarso. Midhowe stalled cairn is the largest intact chambered cairn in

Orkney. The chamber measures 23 by 4m and is divided by 12 pairs of "stalls". About 25 bodies had been laid in a crouched position on or under shelves between the stalls. The outside walls are carefully built with stones set at angles, similar to the designs on *Unstan Ware* pottery.

The Westness Walk takes in the Midhowe Broch, Midhowe Cairn, a Norse farmstead and an excavation at Swandro. The Iron Age broch was occupied from about 200BC to 200AD. Finds included some Roman artefacts, as well as pottery and a bronze ladle. There was evidence of metal working including crucibles, moulds and jewellery.

The site of a Pictish and Viking cemetery lies at Moaness near Westness Farm. Viking brooches, pins, tools and weapons were found, including an elaborate Celtic brooch pin. Boat graves

held the remains of two men wi their weapons, one of whom ha four arrowheads in his body.

There is another broch above t Bay of Swandro. The ruins of Norse Farm are adjacent to th and nearby, on Moaness, there a Norse boat shed and slipwa Skaill is an 18th century far whose tenants were evicted General Burroughs in the 19 century. St Mary's Kirk is t former Rousay parish church. became disused in 1815 after t new church was built. Westne was the most important part Rousay for thousands of yea with continuous settlement sin Neolithic times to the present.

RSPB Reserve The moorlar Trumland RSPB Reserve near t pier is a good place to see He Harriers, Merlin, Peregrine ar Red-throated Divers. The ra *Primula scotica* is found on t maritime heath west coast.

Swandro Chambered Cairn being excavated

Yarso Chambered Cai

Rousay with Egilsay and Wyre in the background and Eynhallow on the right

YRE Cubbie Roo's Castle dates
m the 12th century. It is one of
e oldest and best preserved early
ne built castles in Scotland.
earby the romanesque St Mary's
apel is also Norse. Both are
d to have been built by Kolbein
ruga, a colourful character in
e *Orkneyinga Saga*. His son,
arni, became Bishop of Orkney
1188.

ILSAY was the location of the
artyrdom of Earl Magnus. It
the site of the fine 12th cen-
ry St Magnus Kirk with its
l round tower. A cenotaph
arks the place where the saint is
d to have been killed at Easter
117. Much of Egilsay is an
PB Reserve, managed for the
nefit of wildlife. There are sev-
al lovely secluded sandy coves
the east side. It makes a pleas-
t and peaceful day out. Both
ilsay and Wyre are reached by
e Rousay ferry.

St Magnus Kirk, Egilsay

Midhowe Broch entrance, Westness, Rousay

Cubbie Roo's Castle, Wyre

idhowe Stalled Cairn

ROUSAY

Trumland House
RSPB Trumland Reserve
Midhowe Chambered Cairn
Midhowe Broch
Knowe of Yarso
Blackhammar
Westness Walk
Faraclett Walk
Wyre
Egilsay

WESTRAY (ON *Vestr-ey*, W Isle), often referred to as "T Queen of the Isles", is the seco largest of the North Isles, and many ways could be described "Orkney in miniature". The isla has dramatic cliffs, good beach several ancient sites, and is best place in Orkney to see Puff easily. There are daily roro fe and air services.

Pierowall The village is situa at the head of a sheltered bay the northeast of the island. T excellent harbour was doubtl the reason for its early sett ment. Pictish and Norse grav have been found in the vicin as well as Neolithic and Bron Age remains. Although most the artefacts are either lost in museums elsewhere, some a slowly coming back to Westray.

Archaeology There was Neolithic settlement at the Lir of Noltland, in the sand dun above Grobust beach. These being steadily eroded, reveal much evidence of former habi tion and cultivation. Excavatic in the late 1970s revealed Neolithic house built into t sand. Grooved Ware pottery a many other artefacts were foun

More recently, further work h exposed a large farmhouse w many associated field dykes. 2009 the "Westray Wife", a ti

The Westray W

Noup Head is an RSPB Reserve and a major seabird breeding site

View looking northwest from Skelwick to the Bay of Tuquoy and Fitty Hill

one human female figurine, was found at this site, along with a large number of other artefacts. These include pottery, tools and large numbers of cattle bones. These sites were occupied from about 3000-2000BC.

ruins of several chambered cairns exist, but none are very impressive. At Point of Cott the outline of an excavated cairn can be seen. A carved stone from a destroyed cairn was found at Pierowall and is now in the Westray Heritage Museum.

Broch mounds can be seen at Burrastae and Queena Howe. Westray has been intensively farmed for thousands of years which may possibly explain the relative dearth of prehistoric monuments in good condition. Recent excavations at Quoygrew (Norse) and Knowe o'Skea (Iron Age) have thrown some light on the island's past.

Vikings Quoygrew, on the north side of Rackwick, was partially occupied until 1937. Around AD1000 a building was erected near the shore. Extended many times over the years, this Norse house can now be examined by visitors.

Cross Kirk is on the shore near Tuquoy and dates from the 12th century. It probably belonged to

Noltland Castle was built about 1560

Part of the Pierowall Stone

WESTRAY
Pierowall
Westray Heritage Centre
Noltland Castle
Grobust Beach
Links of Noltland
Quoygrew Norse House
Noup Head
Fitty Hill
Knowe of Skea
Brough of Burrian
Rapness

Grobust Beach lies below Noltland, North Hill and Noup Head are in the background, seen here from the east

Haflidi Thorkelsson of Tuquoy and was dedicated to the Holy Cross. The old part is mostly intact. The remains of a large Viking settlement are eroding out of the shore nearby.

Westray Heritage Centre now prominently hosts the Pierowall Stone as well as other artefacts from recent excavations. Displays are changed annually, but the concentration on nature and the environment continues. There are excellent hands on activities for children and their parents. The large skeleton of a Sperm Whale lies in the garden.

Noltland Castle The gaunt unfinished shell of Noltland Castle overlooks the village. It

was commenced about 1560 by Gilbert Balfour, but never finished. There are fine views from the upper storey. With its many gunloops it has been compared to a ship of the line.

The great hall is spacious, as are the upstairs apartments. However the cavernous kitchen cannot have been very salubrious. The Castle may have been partially habitable as late as 1761, although the roof is said to have been pulled off in 1746 as a result of the Jacobite sympathies of the then owner, Jerome Dennison of Sanday.

Noup Head The landscape more than makes up for lack of ancient sites on display for visitors. The dramatic cliffs at Noup Head

are an RSPB Reserve, which second in numbers of breed seabirds only to St Kilda. A su stantial colony of Gannets is n established.

Puffins In the south the Castle Burrian and surrounding low cl near Rapness Mill is the easi place to see Puffins in Orkn During the breeding season t rock stack and the low cliffs the area are home to many of t cheeky little birds. It is possi to closely observe the Puffins he without disturbance as they p scant attention to humans.

Beaches Sandy beaches a another feature of Westray, w Grobust in the north being p haps the best. Others inclu

Mae Sand

Gannets at Noup Head

Westray and Papay aerial view from the south west, Pierowall lies along the bay at left centre

Rae Sand, Swartmill Bay, Sands o' Woo and Bay of Tafts. There is a sheltered beach for every wind direction. In rough weather it is very exhilarating to take a brisk walk along the sand, watch the waves and look for shells.

Fish & Chips Westray can be visited for a day, but merits at least an overnight stay. The Pierowall Hotel has been recently refurbished and offers *"perhaps the best fish and chips anywhere"*, fresh from the local whitefish fleet, as well as a warm welcome.

Wild Flowers With its diverse range of habitats in a relatively small area, Westray is a good place for the nature enthusiast. The combination of sandy beach-

Cross Kirk at Tuquoy

es, clifftops, maritime heath of the northwest coast (with *Primula scotica*), charming agricultural countryside, unimproved meadows and luxuriant verges the island offers much to botanists.

Transport Westray is served by several direct ferries from Kirkwall daily. Loganair also operate flights from Kirkwall Airport. A small ferry also links Pierowall with Papa Westray, facilitating a visit to both islands.

Puffin at Brough of Burrian

Pierowall fish and chips

Crown copyright

Papay or Papa Westray (ON *Papey hin Meiri*, Big Isle of the Papae), takes its name from the Celtic clergy who were there before the Vikings. This small island lies just east of Westray, across the shallow Papa Sound.

Knap of Howar is the oldest known standing stone built house in Orkney and, like Skara Brae, it was revealed after a severe storm. The walls of the well preserved dwellings still stand to a height of 1.6m, and the stone interiors are remarkably intact.

Large numbers of artefacts including much *Unstan Ware* pottery was found, along with bone, flint and stone tools. Bones of domestic animals, fish, seals and birds, including Great Auk were abundant as well as many mollusc shells. The earliest dates were from about 3600BC, 500 years before Skara Brae, and the latest about 3100BC.

St Boniface Church near the Knap of Howar has been refurbished and is worth a visit. Boniface was a 7th century English missionary who became Archbishop of Germany in AD728, and was massacred with his followers in AD754.

It dates from the 12th century and is still in use today. The interesting grave yard has an 11th century hog backed gravestone which has been dubiously linked to the burial of Earl Rognvald Brusison in c.1045. This site has extensive Iron Age, Pictish and Norse remains, and there was probably a much older chapel here before the Vikings arrived.

Holland Farm has a fine 19th century steading with a circular horse engine house, doocot and corn drying kiln. The main part of the house dates from about 1636, and there is an interesting folk museum in the bothy. Hookin Mill is a 19th century undershot watermill on the shore south of the old pier.

St Tredwell's Chapel is dedicated to St Triduana and is built on top of an Iron Age broch on the east side of Loch of St Tredwell. Triduana was a nun whose eyes, it is said, were so admired by Nechtan, King of Picts, that she plucked them out and sent them to him on a thorn branch to retain her virtue.

North Hill Reserve Papay famous for its birds, and t North Hill RSPB Reserve home to many breeding Te and Arctic Skuas in summ There is a small bird cliff at Fc Craig on the east side, the site the killing of the last Great A in Britain in 1813. They bi here in 1812, when the female w stoned to death for a museum.

The island is also a good place migrants in spring and autum The Mull Head is said to be p haps the best place for sea-wat ing in Orkney, as it forms a n ural turning point. The beach loch and meadows all prov food and cover for migrati waders, waterfowl and passerin

Beaches Like its larger neig bour, Papay has many attract beaches. The shore north of t old pier has fine stretches of sa sheltered from the north a west. Near the south end the are good sandy beaches at t Bay of Moclett and on the w side below Vestness. Between t Knap of Howar and St Bonifa Kirk the shore hides a number lovely little sandy coves.

Holm of Papay has two cha bered cairns, the larger being Maeshowe-type with a chamb over 20m long with 12 side cel This impressive and mostly int structure is well worth a vis Teistie Taing at the south end

St Boniface Kirk dates from the 12th century

11th century hog-backed gravestone at St Bonif

The Knap of Howar is the oldest known house in Orkney, and dates from about 3600BC

good place to see seals and the nearby Bay of South Cruive is good for finding *Groatie Buckies* (cowrie shells).

Flora The North Hill is mostly made up of maritime heath and has an interesting variety of plants, many in dwarf form. These include several sedges and herbs such as Dog Violet, Primrose, Spring Squill, Grass of Parnassus, Heath Spotted Orchid, Mountain Everlasting and *Primula scotica*.

Crofts and fields on the east side of Papay

Shortest Scheduled Flight Papay is connected to Westray by the shortest scheduled air route in the world. The distance of about km (2mi) is undertaken in as little as two minutes, depending on the wind. The flight schedule varies seasonally. The island can also be reached via passenger ferry from Pierowall.

The Shortest Scheduled Flight in the World

Holm of Papay South Chambered Cairn - interior

Papa Westray

Knap of Howar
St Boniface Kirk
St Tredwell's Chapel
Bay of Moclett
Holland Farm
North Hill
Mull Head
South Bay
Holm of Papay
South Cairn on Holm of Papay

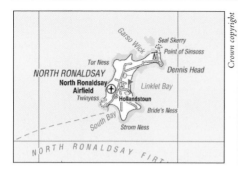

Crown copyright

Kirk Taing, North Ronaldsay and old lighthouse beacon, 17...

NORTH RONALDSAY (ON *Rinansey*, Ringan's or Ninian's Isle) lies to the north east of Sanday, which it resembles with its low lying landscape and sandy beaches. The island has a distinctly different character, and still retains many traditions and language usages now extinct in most of the rest of Orkney. It is the most isolated of the North Isles and is mostly served by air link.

Sheep Dyke This unique feature of the island was built about 1832 to keep the sheep off the agricultural land. The 19km (12mi) drystone dyke encircles the shore. The small, hardy, North Ronaldsay Sheep are similar to Soay sheep, and graze the seaweed off the shore as well as grass on the small areas outside the dyke. The lean meat has a distinctive flavour because of the unique diet.

During lambing time the ew... are allowed onto grass for a tim... Special sheep punds around th... shore are used for clipping a... dipping. The white and brow... fleeces make fine wool, suitable f... knitwear, but the coloured on... are rather coarser.

Most of the houses are renova... ed traditional longhouses, wi... flagstone roofs. The farming he... tends to be less intensive a... more traditional than elsewhe... in Orkney. As a result the island... very attractive to many species... breeding birds in summer.

Bird Observatory (NRB... North Ronaldsay is especially we... situated on a migration crossroa... for birds on passage to northe... breeding grounds in spring a... returning in autumn. Rariti... turn up every year. The NRB... exists to study these movement... It offers guest house and host... accommodation as well as meals...

Fields, farm buildings and Dennis Head, North Ronaldsay

North Ronaldsay Sheep eating seaweed on the shore

North Ronaldsay She...

NORTH RONALDSAY - "RINGAN'S ISLE"

Aerial view of North Ronaldsay from the northwest

Archaeology There are several sites of archaeological interest. These include the Iron Age Broch of Burrian on Strom Ness at the south end. The Stan Stein is a Standing Stone which has a small hole through it in a field near Holland. Traditionally people gathered here at New Year to dance and sing. The Muckle Gairsty and the Matches Dyke are ancient "treb dykes" which divided up the island.

Lighthouse North Ronaldsay lighthouse, at Kirk Taing on Dennis Head, was the first in Orkney, and it was established in 1789. This was the only lighthouse in the North Isles until the Start Point light was built in 1806 on Sanday. The Dennis Head beacon was extinguished in 1809 and its light replaced by the ball of masonry removed from the old Start Point beacon. There are ambitious plans to renovate the beacon and associated houses.

By 1852 the need for a lighthouse was clear and the new brick built lighthouse was first lit in 1854. It was the last one in Orkney to be automated, in 1999. At 42m it is the highest land-based lighthouse in Britain. Dennis Head lighthouse is open to the public by arrangement. The North Ronaldsay Trust owns the outbuildings, some of which now house a small mill to process the local wool. A shop and cafe is open in summer.

Walking North Ronaldsay is low lying and good walking country The circuit of the Sheep Dyke is 19km (12mi) but may be completed in stages. A walk to the lighthouse, from the airfield or pier can take in the whole of this lovely little island. North Ronaldsay will not disappoint, regardless of the season.

Transport It is possible to reach North Ronaldsay by sea from Kirkwall once a week or on a few trip days in summer. These sailings are all weather dependent as the pier is very exposed. Most people travel on the Loganair Islander aircraft from Kirkwall Airport. There are special fares for those staying overnight, but advance booking is essential. The flight offers wonderful views of the North Isles.

North Ronaldsay Lighthouse

Stan Stein - the stone with the hole

Loganair Islander aircraft serve North Ronaldsay

NORTH RONALDSAY

North Ronaldsay Sheep
Sheep Dyke
Bird Observatory
Stan Stein Standing Stone
Dennis Head Old Beacon
North Ronaldsay Lighthouse
Broch of Burrian
Muckle Gairsty Treb Dyke
Hooking Loch
Linklet Bay
South Bay

Midsummer sunrise over Sanday from Wideford Hill

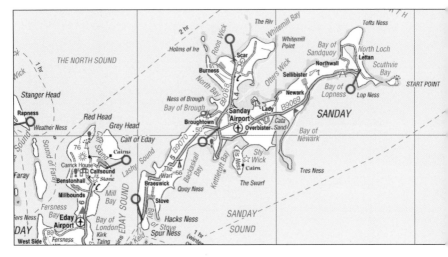

SANDAY (ON *Sand-ey*, Sandy Isle) is the largest of the North Isles. It is very low lying, apart from at the south end, and has many beautiful sandy beaches backed with machair. In summer there is a riot of wild flowers,

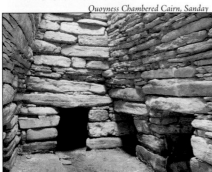

Whalebone plaque from Scar

while the shallow sandy bays are a favourite with the many migrant and resident wading bird species.

Quoyness Chambered Cairn Although there are many sites of archaeological interest, only the Quoyness chambered cairn is actually on display to the public. This impressive Maeshowe-type cairn on the peninsula of Elsness dates from about 3000BC and very much merits a visit. It is largely built from light coloured rounded beach stones, giving the interior a quite special ambience.

Sanday was settled before 4000BC, and the early farmers would have found the light soils easy to till. It was also probably the first to be settled by the

Vikings for the same reason Excavations at Pool have show that occupation was virtually con tinuous from the Neolithic unt post Viking times.

Scar Boat Burial In 1991, a exciting find at Scar was a Vikin boat burial, in which three peopl were interred. A spectacula whalebone plaque was amon the artefacts found. This may b seen, along with other artefacts, a the Orkney Museum in Kirkwal Although the wooden boat ha long since decayed, its shape coul be discerned from iron nails.

Start Point lighthouse was firs lit in 1806, although an unlit bea con had been installed in 1802 The present light was built i

Quoyness Chambered Cairn, Sanday

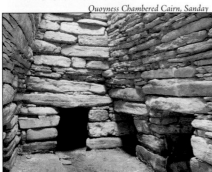

Start Point Lighthouse, Sanda

1870. It is painted with vertical black stripes to distinguish it from North Ronaldsay lighthouse, which has horizontal red stripes. Start Island can be reached at low tide by crossing Ayre Sound.

Radar Station In WWII, Sanday was the only one of the North Isles to have a major military presence. A Chain Home radar station called RAF Whalehead was built at Lopness. Along with its nearby reserve installations and a dummy airfield this brought a good deal of activity to eastern Sanday at the time.

Wildlife The many flat, muddy and sandy beaches, backed by machair, small lochs and marshes are very attractive to waders and waterfowl, both breeders and visitors. Sanday's easterly position, attractive shorelines and relatively large area makes it one of the first landfalls for migrants carried from Europe or America.

Otters frequent the shores and small lochs, and may be seen in the early morning or late evening. Their presence can be noted from the distinctive tracks and fishy spraints which they leave. Many Common Seals live around Sanday, especially off the north coast. Grey Seals breed on the Holms of Ire and Spur Ness.

Flora Sanday is famous for its swards of summer wild flowers.

Backaskaill Bay

Doune Helzie Caves

The low intensity farming, sandy machair soil, lochs and marshes provide a diverse habitat. In midsummer the colours rival any of the Outer Hebrides.

Beaches Sanday is famous for its vast sandy beaches. These include Whitemill Bay, Lopness Bay, Tressness and Cata Sand. The secret coves of Doun Helzie are perhaps the best, with their fantastically eroded sandstone and quiet bays.

Visiting There is plenty of accommodation and facilities on Sanday for visitors. It can be reached daily by sea or air from Kirkwall. With its flat terrain and lovely shoreline, the island is good for walking and cycling. It is easy to underestimate the length of the island, so leave plenty of time to catch your return ferry or flight. An exploration of the southeast shores makes a good short walk. The full tour is at least 40km (25mi).

Lopness Bay with remains of WWI German Destroyer, B98

SANDAY

Quoyness Chambered Cairn
Start Point Lighthouse
B98 WWI destroyer, Lopness
Backaskaill Bay
Whitemill Bay
Lopness Bay
Tres Ness
Bea Loch
North Loch
Kettletoft

Crown copyright

Eday (ON *Eid-ey*, Isthmus Isle) is less fertile than the other outer North Isles and much of it is peaty heather moorland. Its central position means that there are excellent views of much of Orkney from, for example, the top of the Ward Hill, or from the Red Head.

Stone of Setter is 4.5m high and very prominent as it is set in open terrain overlooking Calf Sound and near the Mill Loch, in a focal point of the landscape. The weathered monolith is covered in lichen, which emphasises its time-worn appearance.

Chambered Cairns There are many chambered cairns on the island, some in good condition and some ruinous. Vinquoy, is a Maeshowe-type cairn which overlooks Calf Sound. This interesting structure has been repaired and is built of large sandstone blocks. It has two pairs of side cells and the main chamber is over 3m high inside.

Braeside is a small tripartite cairn whose entrance passage directly faces the Stone of Setter, while the nearby Huntersquoy is on two levels like Taversoe Tuick on Rousay. The upper chamber has largely gone, but the bottom one is intact.

Recent excavations at the south end have revealed a Neolithic settlement. Although there are Bronze Age burnt mounds, so far no brochs, Pictish artefacts or Norse houses have been found.

Carrick House was first built in 1633 and in 1725 nearby Calf Sound was the scene of the capture by its then owner, James Fea, of "Pirate Gow". John Gow was the son of a Stromness merchant, who went to sea. In 1724 he and 5 others mutinied aboard the ship *"Caroline"* off Spain, murdered the officers and proceeded to harry shipping.

Having little success they ended up in Stromness, but the ship was recognised and they sailed to Eday, looking for assistance from Fea, who had been at school with Gow. However Gow and his fellow pirates were captured and he and 7 of his crew were executed in London.

Wildlife The hide on the Mill Loch is a very good place from which to observe Red-throated Divers, and other waterfowl which nest here. Whimbrel, Hen Harrier, Merlins, Arctic Skuas and Short-eared Owls may also be seen on the island during the summer.

Eday Heritage Walk takes in the most interesting sights in the north of the island. It starts at the shop and passes the Mill Loch, Stone of Setter, chambered cairns and Noup Hill, from where there are fine views over the North Isles.

The bright red sandstone here is quite soft and does not erode to form convenient ledges for birds to nest on. A quarry at Fersness is reputed to be one of the main sources of stone for St Magnus Cathedral.

Warness Walk does the same at the south end, starting from Backaland Pier and going round the southwest part of the island. Combined with a pub lunch this is a good between ferries walk.

Calf of Eday lies across Calf Sound from Eday. There are several chambered cairns, including

Calf Sound from the east, Carrick House is mid left

Aerial view of Eday and Stronsay from the north west, Holm of Faray and Faray in foreground

ng a long stalled cairn, a small wo-celled tomb and two intact ookan-type cairns. Opposite Carrick are the remains of a 17th entury saltworks which was peat red. Cormorants and many ther seabirds breed on the island.

eaches There are several very ice beaches. These include, in ne south, the Bay of Greentoft, as ell as the Sands of Doomy and ne Sands of Mussetter. Facing ersness Bay in the northwest. Mill Bay and the Bay of London, the east, are muddy and are specially good for waders.

ransport Eday can be reached aily by ferry from Kirkwall, nd, less frequently, by air from Kirkwall Airport. There is a pub nd accommodation on the island. he ferry schedule allows connections with Stronsay on certain ays.

The Stone of Setter

Carrick House

e Red Head of Eday

Vinquoy Chambered Cairn

EDAY

Stone of Setter
Vinquoy Chambered Cairn
Carrick House
Calf Sound
Mill Loch
Red Head of Eday
Eday Heritage Walk
Warness Walk
Beaches
London Airport
Calf of Eday

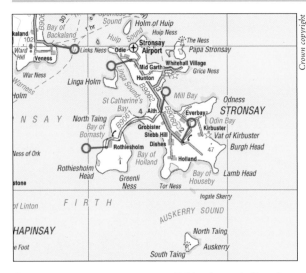

STRONSAY

STRONSAY (ON *Strjonsey*, Profit Island) is one of the most fertile islands in Orkney. It has a much indented coastline, with many very fine beaches, as well as low cliffs on the south east side, with several large caves, and a natural arch at the Vat of Kirbuster. Although most of the island is agricultural land, the headland of Rothiesholm is moorland, thus there is a large variety of habitat and feeding areas for wildlife.

Archaeology There are a number of archaeological sites on the island, but none of great interest, no doubt because it has been intensively farmed for many years. There is a large chambered cairn

at Kelsburgh near the Bu and two smaller ones at Lamb Head.

Herring Stronsay was a major centre for Herring fishing for centuries. The Dutch were fishing in Orkney waters in late Norse times and by the 17th century had over 2,000 boats working the North Sea. The island was used as a harbour for Dutch and Fife boats during the season for hundreds of years up until 1937, when the fishery collapsed.

Whitehall Village was very busy in the fishing season, and once boasted the longest bar in Scotland. On Sundays there were hundreds of boats tied up. The

vast catching power of the stea[m] drifter meant Herring stock[s] were exhausted before WW[I]. Today the harbour is home [to] a few inshore creel boats. Th[e] Fishmarket is now an interpreta[-] tion centre, cafe and hostel. Th[e] Stronsay Hotel in Whitehall h[as] recently been renovated and offe[rs] food and accommodation.

Kelp-making was introduced [to] Stronsay about 1719, to mak[e] potash and soda, which were use[d] in glass and soap manufactu[re] and were in short supply due [to] the French Wars. Kelp was pro[-] duced by burning dried seawee[d] in pits on the shore. The expan[-] sive beaches in the North Isl[es] were excellent sources of seawee[d] which had traditionally been car[ri-] ed onto the land as fertiliser. A[t] the peak, Orkney was exporti[ng] 3,000 tons of kelp per year.

The boom lasted from 1780 [to] 1830, and brought much wealt[h] to the landowners, some of whic[h] was invested in farm improve[-] ments. Kelp pits can be see[n] round the shore, especially Grice Ness, east of Whitehall.

Beaches On Stronsay there is [a] beach for every wind directio[n]. St Catherine's Bay, the Bay [of] Holland, the Bay of Huip an[d] Mill Bay have the largest expans[e] of sand, but there are many oth[er] small beaches to explore.

The Vat of Kirbuster is a lar[ge] natural arch and gloup forme[d] from a collapsed cave. The coas[t] line here has several large an[d] interesting caves which can b[e] explored with a small boat.

Papa Stronsay, now occupi[ed] by Transalpine Redemptori[st] Monks, has a chambered cair[n] the "Earl's Knowe", and a chap[el] site, dedicated to St Nichol[as]. The church excavated some yea[rs]

The Vat of Kirbuster - a collapsed cave

Stronsay, aerial view from the south

ago dates from the 11th century, but the site may go back to the 8th century or even earlier.

Wildlife Stronsay is an excellent island for birdwatching, being well sited to attract migrants in spring and autumn. The diverse range of habitats attract many unusual bird species at times. Grey Seals haul ashore to pup at several places around the island, with large numbers on Links Ness and on Linga Holm, as well as on Grice Ness, Odness and Lamb Head. Common Seals are also .present.

Walking and Cycling Being flat, the island offers easy walking and cycling, with several waymarked

official trails. These include Odin Bay to Houseby, Sand of Rothiesholm and Baywest, St Catherine's Bay, Grice Ness and Holland Farm to Torness.

Transport Stronsay can be reached daily by roro ferry and by air from Kirkwall. A bicycle would allow most places to be visted between ferries.

Whitehall Village from the West Pier

Whitehall Village from the East Pier

STRONSAY
Whitehall Village
Herring Fishing (Fishmarket)
St Catherine's Bay
Bay of Holland
Mill Bay
Lamb Head
Vat of Kirbuster
Rothiesholm
Grice Ness, Grey Seals
Linga Holm
Papa Stronsay

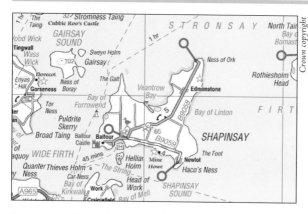

Crown copyright

Shapinsay (ON *Hjalpand-isey*, Helping Island) is only 20 minutes from Kirkwall by roro ferry. It was one of the first areas where the old runrig system was changed to larger fields, and is nearly all cultivated today.

Broch of Burroughston This is the only archaeological site which is on display, having been excavated in 1862. It is surrounded by a ditch and rampart, and has a well-preserved interior, nearly 3m high inside. There is an intact corbelled cell in the entrance passage and a large central well accessed by steps.

Mor Stane The 3m Mor Stane is of indeterminate date and is said to have been thrown by a giant from the Mainland at his departing wife. On the north side below Lairo Water, Odin's Stone may have been a Norse meeting place.

Norse Power Shapinsay featured in the unsuccessful bid by King Haakon of Norway to reassert Norse power in the west of Scotland in 1263. The great fleet was mustered here in Elwick Bay, before its departure for the Clyde.

Balfour Castle The house of Sound was built in 1674 by Arthur Buchanan, on the site of the present Balfour Castle. In 1775 Thomas Balfour married Frances Liginier, whose money paid for the Sound Estate. Soon the island was transformed with a new house, Cliffdale, the village, then called Shoreside, farm buildings and dykes all being built.

In 1846 David Balfour, who had made a fortune in India, inherited the estate, which now included the whole island. He had the house transformed into the present building. The Castle interior has not changed much in 150 years with most of the original furnishing and interior decor still in place.

RSPB Milldam Reserve The disused Elwick Mill is one of the largest water mills in Orkney, and the artificial loch behind it is now the RSPB Mill Dam Reserve. There are fine views of many kinds of waders and waterfowl from the hide on its west side. The lochs of Lairo Water and Vasa are also fine places for birds. The tidal Ouse and mudflats of Veantrow Bay are good for waders.

Beaches The island boasts a number of fine sandy beaches including Skenstoft, Sandside, Innsker, Noust of Erraby and Sandy Geo on the north side. The best is probably the south-facing Bay of Sandgarth in the southeast corner of the island, said to be the Shapinsay folk's favourite.

Walks Shapinsay is one of the easiest of islands to visit from Kirkwall. A walking or cycling tour round the whole island would take an entire day, making a fine introduction to one of the North Isles.

MV "Shapinsay"

Sunset over the Wide Firth

Elwick Bay and Balfour Village, with Balfour Castle in the background, Shapinsay

Helliar Holm is on the south side of Elwick Bay. Many Common Seals lie up on the flat rocks of the bay. There is a chambered cairn at the highest point of the island. The lighthouse was built in 1893 to guide the eastern approach to Kirkwall Bay. In former times

there was a fishing station near the present jetty.

Thieves Holm The ferry passes this little island on the way to Shapinsay. In former times convicts were banished here, being tied to a post and left to die.

Transport Shapinsay makes a pleasant short excursion from Kirkwall on the ferry which runs back and fore all day. There is an excellent restaurant, the Smithy in the village. B&B accommodation is available on the island.

The Mor Stane

Burroughston Broch

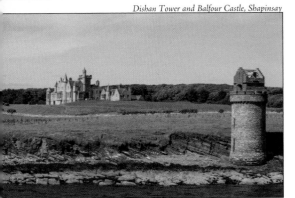

Dishan Tower and Balfour Castle, Shapinsay

Shapinsay

Balfour Castle
Balfour Village
The Smiddy Heritage Centre
RSPB Milldam Reserve
Elwick Mill Pottery
Broch of Burroughston
Odin's Stone
Mor Stone
Elwick Bay
Helliar Holm
Lochs
Beaches

Atlantic Puffin (Tammy Norie)

Loganair SAAB 340 in FlyBe colours at Kirkwall Airport

GETTING TO ORKNEY

Although apparently isolated, Orkney is very well served by transport links. There are good daily year-round connections by air from all four major airports in Scotland. Ferries run several times daily to Caithness and several times per week to Aberdeen and Shetland.

AIR ROUTES Today it is not necessary to go to the lengths that the first airborne visitors had to. In 1910, the author's grandfather was surprised to find two young Germans from Munich on his doorstep. They had gone for a balloon flight, hoping to reach Switzerland. Much to their consternation the weather changed and they crossed the North Sea, landing at the back of Park Cottage, Kirkwall, after seeing the lights of the town!

Kirkwall Airport (Grimsetter) is open seven days per week and is equipped with an Instrument Landing System, which greatly improves the reliability of flights in adverse weather conditions. The airport is about 4km (3mi) east of the town, and is easily reached by taxi or scheduled bus.

Loganair operate several flights into Kirkwall Airport (KOI) every day, from Aberdeen, Inverness, Edinburgh and Glasgow. There are also daily flights to and from Shetland. Loganair use Saab 340 aircraft which carry 34 passengers with a cruising speed of 250kt at 20,000ft. Loganair has a codesharing agreement with BA for onwards flights.

Loganair Flight Details, information and bookings can be found online, or by calling
Tel 0344 800 2855
loganair.com

Loganair Internal Flights Information can also be had from the Loganair desk at Kirkwall Airport.
Tel 01856 872494

British Airways
General Reservations and Enquiries
Tel 0844 493 0787
ba.com
(Note: BA can only assist when the booking is on a codeshare flight with a direct connection to a BA service)

Kirkwall Airport is operated by HIAL
Information Desk
Tel 01856 886210
Live flight information at
hial.co.uk/kirkwall-airport

ADS (Air Discount Scheme)
Reservations and Assistance
Tel   0844 800 2855
   Mon-Fri 0700-1700
Tel   01496 302022
flybe.com/ads

SEA ROUTES The main routes are from Stromness to Scrabster, St Margaret's Hope to Gills Bay and Kirkwall to Aberdeen and Lerwick. There is also a passenger ferry in summer from Burwick to John o' Groats. All sailings are subject to weather conditions and disruption due to storms can occur in winter especially.

Serco NorthLink Ferries currently operate MV *Hamnavoe* between Scrabster in Caithness and Stromness. This large ferry takes about 1½ hours to cross the Pentland Firth, passing the Old Man of Hoy on the way. NorthLink also operate MV *Hjaltland* and MV *Hrossey*, which run between Aberdeen, Kirkwall and Lerwick.

MV "Hrossey" at Hatston Terminal, Kirkwall on a midsummer evening

erco NorthLink Ferries,
erry Terminal, Stromness,
rkney KW16 £2BH
eservations 0845 6000 449
dmin 01856 885500
ax 01856 851795
orthlinkferries.co.uk

entland Ferries operate year-
ound services from St Margaret's
lope to Gills Bay in Caithness
ith MV *Pentalina*, a large cata-
aran. The scenic trip takes
bout 1 hour.

entland Ferries Ltd, Pier Road,
t Margaret's Hope, Orkney
W17 2SW
el 01856 831226
ax 01856 831614
entlandferries.co.uk

ohn o' Groats Ferries run a sum-
er passenger service between
ohn o' Groats and Burwick in
outh Ronaldsay with MV
entland Venture. There are coach
ervices to Kirkwall. A special bus
ervice from Inverness connects
ith the ferry. Several variations
n day trips are available.

ohn o' Groats Ferries, John o'
iroats, Caithness KW1 4YR
el 01955 611353
ax 01955 611301
gferry.co.uk

ETTING TO SCRABSTER The
A9 trunk road north from Perth
not a good road, and it takes at
east 6 hours to drive the 300km
250mi) north from Edinburgh
r Glasgow. Care needs to be
aken on this section of the A9
which has some short sections of
ual carriageway. The road north
f Inverness is very scenic and
ess busy, though still tortuous
n places. There are plenty of
ood hotels and B&Bs to stay in
Caithness overnight, and indeed
ome time exploring this area is
trongly recommended.

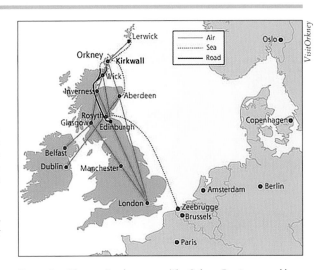

VisitOrkney

BUSES AND TRAINS Land transport links from Edinburgh and
Glasgow to Aberdeen and Thurso
are operated by Scottish CityLink
and by First ScotRail. Details of
services and timetables are available from the companies.

Scottish Citylink Coaches Ltd,
Buchanan Bus Station,
Killermont St,
Glasgow G2 3NP
Tel 08705 505050
Fax 0141 332 4488
citylink.co.uk

First ScotRail
Customer Relations,
PO BOX 7030
Fort William PH33 6WX
Tel 0844 556 5636
scotrail.co.uk

The Orkney Bus is operated by
Stagecoach in the Highlands
Inverness Bus Station,
Farraline Park,
Inverness IV1 1LT
Tel 01463 258933
stagecoachbus.com

Connections There are coach
connections between Thurso
train station and Scrabster as
well as between Wick and Gills
Bay. Citylink buses also meet
some sailings of the Hamnavoe.
It should be noted that the timetables are not always synchronised
and thus it is important to check
out such expected connections in
advance. All of the times may
be checked out on the websites
listed here.

MV "Pentalina" in Hoxa Sound en route for Gills Bay

VisitOrkney

All services are roro except tho[se] to Papay, North Ronaldsay ar[d] Graemsay, where vehicles a[re] handled by crane. The mode[rn] fleet of ships runs frequent da[ily] services to all islands exce[pt] North Ronaldsay, which is on[ce] or twice weekly. The services ru[n] as follows:

Outer North Isles services depa[rt] from Kirkwall for Westray, Pap[a] Westray, Eday, Sanday, Strons[ay] and North Ronaldsay.
To book Tel 01856 872044

Rousay, Egilsay & Wyre servic[es] depart from Tingwall in Evie.
To book Tel 01856 751360

Papay services depart fro[m] Pierowall, Westray.
To book Tel 01857 677216

Hoy and Flotta services depa[rt] from Houton in Orphir.
To book Tel 01856 811397

North Hoy & Graemsay servic[es] depart from Stromness.
To book Tel 01856 850624

ISLAND VISITS A trip to Orkney is not complete without a visit to one or more of the islands, as well as visiting all the interesting places on the Mainland. Since each island is different, with its own charm, and the inter island transport system is good, it is both easy and interesting to visit all of the islands as well as the Mainland parishes.

INTER ISLAND FERRY TRANSPORT The main internal sea transport operator is Orkney Ferries, which operates to most inhabited Islands from Kirkwall, Tingwall, Houton and Stromness. They publish an annual timetable with details of services. Further information from the head office at the Pierhead, Kirkwall Tel 01856 872044.

Fares There are two levels [of] fares to the islands. Tickets f[or] the inner islands of Hoy, Flott[a,] Rousay, Egilsay, Wyre an[d] Shapinsay are cheaper than thos[e] to the Outer Isles of Westra[y,] Eday, Sanday, Stronsay an[d] North Ronaldsay.

Orkney Ferries vessels at Kirkwall Pier

Internal Air Services

Loganair operate daily services to most of the Outer North Isles with 8-seat Islander aircraft. These include Westray, Papay, North Ronaldsay, Sanday and Stronsay and to Eday on Wednesdays only. Flying from Kirkwall airport, these services are very popular, and booking is generally required.

Special deals exist for visitors to Papay and North Ronaldsay if an overnight stay is included.

Loganair Internal Flights

Bookings and Inquiries:
Tel 01856 872494 or 873457
Mon-Sat 0815-1745
Sun 1330-1630
Fax 01856 872420
loganair.co.uk

Public Transport

Stagecoach is the main bus operator in Orkney. They run a large number of services between Kirkwall and Stromness, to ferry terminals and various locations on the Mainland.

Public Transport Timetable. Full details of all these and other schedules are published by Orkney Islands Council every six months in the Orkney Public Transport Timetable. This booklet is indispensable to anyone wishing to make best use of the complexity of routes and times.

Car Hire Orkney is very much a car-orientated society, and independent transport makes it much easier to see the areas not served by public transport. Several firms have cars for hire, including on many of the islands.

Taxis Taxis are available throughout Orkney, either for normal hires, or tours. See advertisements for telephone numbers. Please check in *"The Orcadian"*

A Loganair "Islander" aircraft

or ask at the Tourist Office for further information. There are taxi ranks at the Pier Head, Broad Street and the Airport in Kirkwall and in Stromness at the Pier Head. Taxis may also be ordered to meet ferries, etc.

Bicycle Hire Orkney, being relatively flat, is good country for cycling, but note the wind direction before setting off, it could be much harder getting back! On a nice day there is no better way to absorb the rhythm of the countryside than from a bike. Bicycles may be hired in Kirkwall and in Stromness as well as on several of the islands.

Tours of Orkney Apart from the Maxi Tours offered by John o' Groats Ferries, smaller operators offer tours on the Mainland and several of the islands. Check with VisitOrkney, or locally, for the tours currently being run.

Fresson Memorial, Kirkwall Airport

John o' Groats Ferries tour bus at Brodgar

Clydesdale horses at work at a ploughing match in Firth

VISITOR FACILITIES Orkney has a diverse range of accommodation available to suit every taste and budget. The full range is published in the annual Orkney Tourist Guide produced by the Orkney Tourism Group (OTG). The *"Islands of Orkney"* brochure produced by Orkney Ferries also has listings of North and South Isles facilities. The website visitorkney.com lists all members of OTG.

In recent years there has been a large investment in upgrading of existing accommodation, as well as a large number of new self-catering establishments.

Hotels range from four star town establishments to three star coun-

Carting "ware" from the shore

try inns. There are also more basic, yet comfortable, hotels on most of the islands. Although most of the hotels are in Kirkwall and Stromness, there are several attractive establishments in country locations.

Bed and Breakfast accommodation is available throughout Orkney and on most of the inhabited islands. Although most of the establishments in Kirkwall and Stromness are part of the VisitScotland grading scheme, many of the islands businesses are not.

Self Catering accommodation is by far the most popular choice for visitors coming to stay for one or two weeks, with over 500 units

available. These range from five star town and country premises to basic cottages.

Properties include everything from beautifully renovated mills, new build apartments, chalets and old houses in idyllic locations to rustic simplicity. A complete range is available from luxurious five star accommodation to ungraded, yet comfortable, cottages in remote landscapes.

Hostels Orkney Islands Council has some fine hostels in old schools. The Birsay Hostel is near Palace Village, while on Hoy there is one near the Moaness Pier and another in Rackwick. There are private hostels in places which include Kirkwall, Stromness, South Ronaldsay, Rousay, Sanday and North Ronaldsay.

Camp Sites Apart from the two Council-run camp sites in Kirkwall and Stromness, Orkney is poorly provisioned for campers. Wild camping is possible in many places, but the permission of the landowner needs to be sought first. Public toilets are universally well-kept and are plenty scattered around the islands. There are a number of small private camping sites.

Accommodation Booking The annual brochures produced by the Tourism Group, Orkney Ferries, Shipping Companies and others provide basic information about many establishments. The best sources are the websites of the individual operators. Some offer online booking and availability, while others require a phone call or email.

Eating Out Orkney offers a wide range of establishments serving food and drink. These include everything from outstanding award winning restaurants to chip shops. Most take advantage of high quality local produce when possible, especially beef, lamb and seafood.

Although most of the hotels, cafes and restaurants are situated in and around Kirkwall and Stromness, there are many establishments serving the outlying parishes and islands. To avoid disappointment advance booking is recommended. In remoter places it is advisable to check opening hours locally.

Food Shopping Apart from the ubiquitous Tesco, Lidl and Cooperative supermarkets, Orkney has a wide variety of local food shops. These range from world class butchers to small island shops. While the former are essential to all meat-loving visitors, the latter are timeless examples of what shopping used to be like. The range and quality of stock in many of these remote emporiums may surprise many who are new to such civilised "retail therapy".

It is also a good idea to check locally about whether seafood may be available from friendly fishermen. In season there are several small market gardens which supply local shops with fruit and vegetables far superior to those shipped in. The tomatoes and strawberries are recommended.

Taking in the harvest in the 1920s

Kirkwall Harbour Basin in the 1890s

Grinding corn with a quernstone

Kirkwall in around 1900

The Ba' is played every Christmas and New Year's Day in Kirkwall

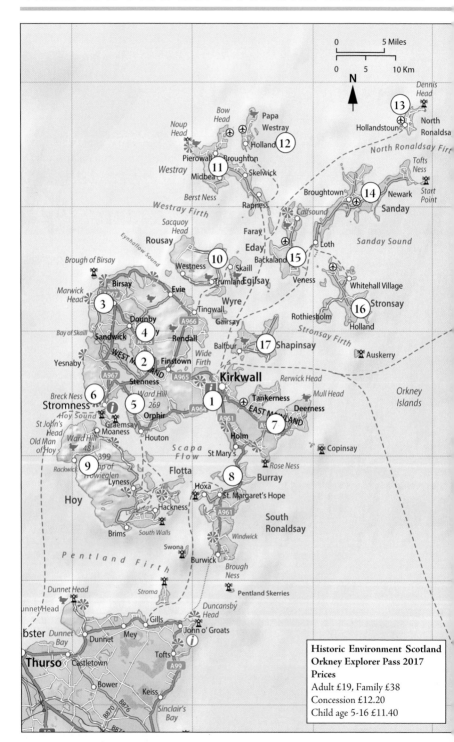

Historic Environment Scotland
Orkney Explorer Pass 2017
Prices
Adult £19, Family £38
Concession £12.20
Child age 5-16 £11.40

WHAT TO DO AND SEE - SOME SUGGESTED ITINERARIES

WHAT TO DO AND SEE A selection of suggested itineraries is included in the following pages. These cover all of the main sites of interest, on the Mainland as well as the North and South Isles. Each excursion is designed to take a day, with plenty of time for getting there, exploration and a picnic or meal along the way.

Private Transport The itineraries here all assume the use of a car to visit the places mentioned during the course of a day. Many could also be done by bicycle or by a combination of public transport and walking. Do not underestimate the distances involved. Orkney is bigger than it first appears.

Public Transport Many of the places mentioned can be reached by public transport, during the summer. However buses to the less frequented places may be infrequent.

THE ORKNEY GUIDE BOOK 4TH EDITION includes full information on all of the sites mentioned in these itineraries. **THE ORKNEY PEEDIE GUIDE 4TH EDITION (REVISED)** is intended for use in the field and includes all of the itineraries from the main guide. The Peedie Guide is designed for those on short visits or who do not wish to carry the main book everywhere.

Itineraries Each Itinerary gives the location, opening hours, distances and estimated time to allow for each place of interest. In general manned Historic Scotland sites and private visitor attractions have an entry charge. Council properties, art galleries and craft businesses are generally free to enter.

All of the unmanned monuments are open at all times. This means that they can be visited at the best times of day for lighting conditions and when the crowds have left.

The Tomb of the Eagles is one of many fascinating Visitor Attractions

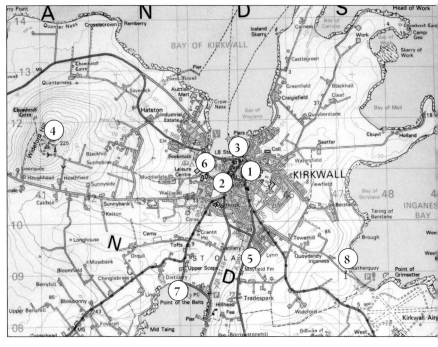

Kirkwall (ON *Kirkjuvagr*, Church Bay), as the main settlement in Orkney, is a good starting point for a visit to the islands. It is first mentioned in the Orkneyinga Saga. It was the dwelling place of Earl Rognvald Brusison about 1035, who built a church dedicated to King Olav of Norway there. Later, the town developed around the Cathedral, and became the administrative and commercial centre. Its access to the North Isles, central position and sheltered harbour in the, then much bigger, Peedie Sea made it an obvious location.

Today the winding main Street still follows the shape of the original settlement. Many of the old houses with end-on gables date from the 16th to 18th centuries. Narrow lanes run off the Street which has many attractive shops. At Broad Street it opens into the expanse of the grass covered Kirk Green in front of St Magnus Cathedral.

The harbour front is the scene of much activity with ferries, fishing boats and, in summer, cruise ships. Over the last 200 years the pier has greatly expanded, yet still retains much of its charm. The marina is home to pleasure craft and is visited by many yachts in the summer. Occasionally one or more tall ships lends a taste of nostalgia to the scene.

Kirkwall & St Ola

Bowling Green
Earl's & Bishop's Palaces
Fusion Nightclub
Golf Course
Harbour and Basin area
Highland Park Distillery
Old St Olaf's Kirk
Orkney Library & Archives
Orkney Museum
Peedie Sea
Pickaquoy Centre
St Magnus Cathedral
St Magnus Centre
The Reel (Wrigley Sisters)
The Street
Town Hall
Wireless Museum

West

Wideford Hill
Wideford Hill Chambered Cairn
Hatston Airfield (WWII)
Grain Earthhouse

South

Scapa Beach & Bay
Scapa Distillery
Lingro Broch (site of)

East

Highland Park Distillery
Head of Work
Head of Holland
Inganess Bay
Bay of Meil
Grimsetter Airport

ORDNANCE SURVEY 1:50,000 & 1:25,000 MAPS OF KIRKWALL

OS Landranger Map 6	Orkney - Mainland
OS Explorer Map 461	Orkney - East Mainland
Nicholson	Kirkwall Street Map 1:14,000

1. KIRKWALL & ST OLA (PAGES 12-17)

A pedestrian day around Kirkwall and St Ola. A car, buses or taxis could be used to shorten some of the walks if time is limited. The town has a large variety of places for refreshment, from small cafes to excellent restaurants. The Street is home to an interesting and wide selection of quality local shops, with hardly a chain store in sight.

1. St Magnus Cathedral (page 14, *opening hours, no charge*) is an essential visit on even the shortest of tours. This ancient Norse church is austere on the outside, but inspiringly beautiful inside. The colourful sandstone, Norman arches and later additions make for a coherently lovely church, which is the pride of Orkney, and uniquely belongs to the people.

2. Orkney Museum (page 12, *opening hours, no charge*) is across the road from the Cathedral and provides a very good introduction to Orkney's cultural heritage. This museum is in Tankerness House, which originally housed church officials. It covers Orkney from the Neolithic Age to the present.

The Earl's Palace and Bishop's Palace (page 12 *Historic Scotland, opening hours, admission charge*) are opposite the Cathedral. The former mostly dates from the 16th century, while the latter was built at the end of that century by the discredited, and executed, Patrick Stewart. There is a fine view of the town from the top of the Moosie Too'er.

Orkney Library & Archives on Junction Road has free Internet facilities as well as the usual lending services. The Orkney Archive should be the first stop for those investigating their family history 200m from Broad Street, Tel 01856 873166).

3. The Street and Harbour (page 12) A walk down the Street in Kirkwall is both a trip into the past and the future. The Street follows the old shoreline and has many old houses. It also has a plentitude of interesting shops, with very few chain stores. A retail therapy paradise.

4. Wideford Hill (page 13, 225m) is a very good viewpoint from which to take in Kirkwall, the North Isles, Scapa Flow and, to the south, Scotland (8km, 5mi, 90min return from Broad Street).

5. Highland Park Visitor Centre (page 13 *opening hours, admission charge*) is on the Holm Road on the southeast side of the town. Tours include an interesting audiovisual display and a tasting of the single malt. Connoisseur and even more special Magnus Eunson in-depth Tours are available (1,500m from Broad Street, 60min for tour, Tel 01856 874619).

6. The Peedie Sea is the remains of Kirkwall Oyce that in former times was open to the sea. The Street follows the former shore line. Gulls, seaducks, waders and swans are attracted here; it offers close views. A circuit makes a fine walk, perhaps combined with the harbour area (1,000m, 60min).

Pickaquoy Centre (*opening hours, charges for some events, movies and for use of facilities*) is a multipurpose sports, arts and leisure facility next to the Peedie Sea. It incorporates the Phoenix Cinema, a Fitness Suite, Swimming Pools, Squash Courts and other facilities. The Pickaquoy Caravan and Camping Park is next to it (700m from Broad Street Tel 01856 87 9900).

7. Scapa Beach and Bay (page 13) is about 2km from Broad Street. A pleasant walk from Kirkwall follows the A963 and B9148 south from Kirkwall. A footpath through Crantit Valley leads to Scapa Beach. Return via the road after exploring the beach. Alternatives include taking the footpath along the low cliffs past the waterfall at the west end of the bay to Dyke End, then returning via the Bloomfield Road and Wideford Hill. Walk 8 starts from the east end of the beach (6km, 4mi, 2h from Broad Street).

Scapa Distillery Visitor Centre (page 13 *opening hours, admission charge*) is signposted off the A964 and overlooks Scapa Bay. This artisanal, manually operated distillery has the only Lomond still in Scotland. After a tour of the distillery, visitors can taste a Scapa expression, available to buy in the gift shop (3km, 2mi) from Broad Street, 60min for tour, Tel 01856 873269).

8. Wideford Burn & Inganess Bay This fine walk along a bridleway and footpaths starts near Scapa Pier, crosses the A961 and then follows the course of the Wideford Burn to another fine beach at Inganess Bay (4km, 2.5mi, 60min). Return to Kirkwall via the side road from Inganess (3km, 2mi, 40min).

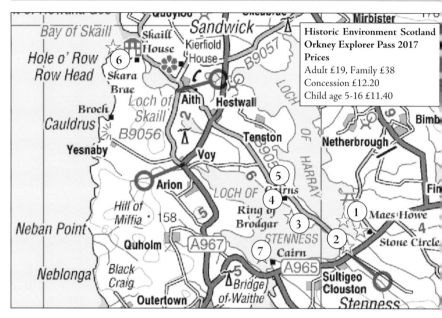

Historic Environment Scotland
Orkney Explorer Pass 2017
Prices
Adult £19, Family £38
Concession £12.20
Child age 5-16 £11.40

The Heart Of Neolithic Orkney

The Heart Of Neolithic Orkney The term "Neolithic" (Greek neos, new and lithos, stone) was coined by Sir John Lubbock in 1865. It covers the period from c.10000-2000BC during which agriculture, buildings, settlements, writing, weaving, pottery making and much else developed. From the first domesticated crops being grown in the Middle East around 10000BC to the oldest known house in Orkney is about 6,000 years.

Today Orkney retains a vas archaeological treasury of build ings, artefacts and evidence fron this time. In recognition of thi "The Heart of Neolithic Orkney was inscribed on the Worl Heritage List by UNESCO i 1999. Because of their outstand ing universal value, "The monu ments of Orkney, dating back t 3000-2000BC, are outstandin testimony to the cultural achieve ments of the Neolithic peoples o northern Europe."

This tour covers all of the mai monuments in this group, as we as several nearby subsidiary site which should be visited if tim allows. Visits to Maeshowe mus be booked in advance online Tours start from the Visito Centre in Stenness.

Skara Brae should probably b avoided during the main part o the day when cruise liners are i Kirkwall. In general all of thes monuments are best appreciate during times of year regarded b some as "out of season".

The Heart Of Neolithic Orkney

Neolithic Timeline		Places To See
BC		
c.11000	Pentland Firth flooded	Maeshowe
c.8000	First hunter-gatherers?	Standing Stones of Stenness
c.3600	Knap of Howar oldest date	Barnhouse Stone
	Unstan Ware pottery	Barnhouse Village
c.3200	Stalled cairns appear	Watchstone
	Isbister oldest date	Odinstone (site of)
	Maeshowe tombs appear	Ness of Brodgar
	Skara Brae oldest date	Ring of Brodgar
	Ness of Brodgar earliest	Comet Stone
c.3100	Knap of Howar latest	Dyke o' Sean
	Quanterness Cairn	Ring of Bookan
	Grooved Ware pottery	Skara Brae
c.3000	Standing Stones	Skaill House
	Quoyness Cairn	Bay of Skaill
	Skara Brae phase II	Unstan Cairn
c.2800	Maeshowe built	Orkney Museum, Kirkwall
c.2700	Ring of Brodgar built	Stromness Museum
c.2600	Woodland virtually gone	
c.2500	Cairns latest date	
	Skara Brae latest	
c.2200	Ness of Brodgar latest	

---

2. The Heart of Neolithic Orkney (pages 20-31)

his tour can be started at Maeshowe and timed o suit the tour booked. The total distance is about 4km (15mi) return to Maeshowe, with an optional xtra 5km (3mi) detour to Unstan. There is a cafe nd toilets at Skara Brae (toilets at Tormiston Mill).

Maeshowe (page 30, *opening hours, hourly tours om Visitor Centre, admission charge, online booking equired*) should preferably be visited first. In midinter 1400 is best for the sunset; in midsummer here are evening openings. Advance booking essenal, (bus from Visitor Centre, 400m walk, 60min).

The Standing Stones of Stenness (page 28, *pen at all times, no charge*) are most impressive in arly morning or evening light. At the south end f the Bridge of Brodgar, the **Watchstone** stands entinel over the landscape. The **Odinstone**, which *vas* destroyed in 1814, stood between it and the tanding Stones.

Barnhouse Village (page 29, *open at all times, no barge*)is about 300m along a path leading towards he Loch of Stenness. The footings of several buildngs are marked out. **Barnhouse Stone** can be best een from the side road to Stenness Kirk.

Ness of Brodgar (page 26, *open during annual xcavation period no charge, tours by Rangers*) is ver Brodgar Bridge on the B9055. Several large Neolithic structures are being excavated here. Apart rom the buildings, two large walls divide the site rom the surrounding ground. The site should not e missed when it is open and it is well worthwhile aking one of the guided tours (100m, 60min).

Ring of Brodgar (page 24, *open at all times, no harge, tours by Rangers daily in summer, weekly in vinter, weather permitting*) has a large carpark about 00m from the circle. Even if time is limited a valk around the stones is completely essential. The earby Salt Knowe and Comet Stone should also be isited (extra 500m). The Ring of Brodgar is at its est in morning or evening light (1,000m, 60min).

5. The Dyke o' Sean winds across the Ness of Brodgar, from beside the carpark to a mound on the shore of the Loch of Stenness. This ancient wall has been the Stenness/Sandwick parish boundary since time immemorial. It crosses the marshy field with the Brodgar Pools, which are excellent for waders and waterfowl in all seasons.

The Ring of Bookan (page 292) is well worth a visit, especially around the solstices. Park considerately and explore the ring with its chambered cairn and the Skae Frue mound. The Bookan chambered cairn is about 500m to the south, near ancient quarry workings (1,500, 60min).

6. Skara Brae (page 22, *opening hours, admission charge, joint ticketing with Skaill House, Tel 01856 841815*) is considered by many to be the Jewel in the Crown of Orkney's archaeology. It is certainly an essential visit. The Visitor Centre has a short audiovisual programme, museum and a replica of hut 7. These should be the first stop, before going to the village itself. On the way note the date tablets. Skara Brae itself has a number of convenient viewing places with interpretation panels. Please note that hut 7 cannot currently be seen because the glass roof has been grassed over. (Skara Brae is a 400m walk from the Visitor Centre, and about 8km, 5mi from the Ring of Brodgar).

Skaill House (page 38, *opening hours, admission charge, joint ticketing with Skara Brae*) is adjacent, and is the only such house in Orkney open to the public (300m from Skara Brae, 60min).

7. Unstan Chambered Cairn (*p38, free entry*) is situated off the A965 near the Brig of Waithe. This visit makes a short detour from the Standing Stones. The cairn is similar to the Tomb of the Eagles in South Ronaldsay and should be visited if there is not time to reach the latter. This tomb is where *Unstan Ware* was first found and is an interesting hybrid type with stone stalls in the main chamber and a small cell opposite the entrance passage (400m walk, 6km, 4mi, 30min).

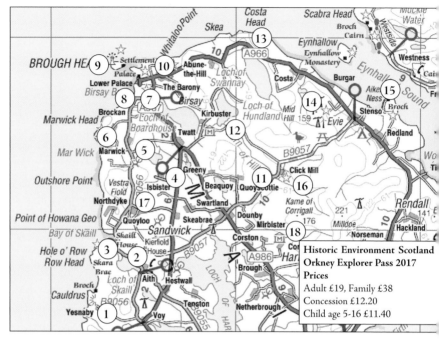

Historic Environment Scotland
Orkney Explorer Pass 2017
Prices
Adult £19, Family £38
Concession £12.20
Child age 5-16 £11.40

WEST MAINLAND The parishes of Sandwick, Birsay and Evie include many of Orkney's most popular attractions, including archaeology, historical sites, stunning coastal scenery and landscapes as well as many bir and wild flowers.

SANDWICK, BIRSAY, EVIE & HARRAY

SANDWICK

BAY OF SKAILL AREA

Bay of Skaill
Knowe o' Snusgar
Loch of Skaill
Skaill House
Skara Brae
St Peter's Kirk

SOUTH TO STROMNESS

Broch of Borwick
Brough of Bigging
Hole o' Row
Primula scotica
Row Head
Walk South to Stromness
Yesnaby

NORTH TO BIRSAY

Cruaday Quarry
Northdyke
Quoyloo (Orkney Brewery)
Vestrafiold Monoliths
Walk North to Birsay

INLAND

Broch of Stackrue
Dyke o' Sean
Loch of Clumley and Broch
Ring of Bookan
Skeabrae
Stones of Via
Voy

BIRSAY

Barony Mills
Birsay Bay
Birsay Links
Brough of Birsay
Costa Head & Hill
Cruaday Quarry
Earl's Palace
Groatie Buckies
Kirbuster Museum
Kitchener Memorial
Loch of Boardhouse
Loch of Hundland
Loch of Swannay
Marwick Head
Northside

Oxtro Broch
Point of Buckquoy
RSPB Birsay Moors
RSPB Marwick Head
RSPB The Loons
Skipi Geo
St Magnus Kirk
Stone of Quoybune
Twatt Airfield
Vestrafiold

EVIE

Aerogenerators
Birsay Moors RSPB
Broch of Burgar
Broch of Gurness
Burgar Hill
Costa Head
Eynhallow Sound
Hillside Road
Lowrie's Water
Sands of Aikerness
Woodwick

ORDNANCE SURVEY 1:50,000 AND 1:25,000 MAPS

OS Landranger Map 6   Orkney - Mainland
OS Explorer Map 463   Orkney - West Mainland

---

3. Sandwick, Birsay, Evie & Harray (pages 34-39)

. Yesnaby is about 7km (4.5mi) south of the Bay f Skaill and has some of the most stunning cliff cenery in Orkney, with fine walks to the north nd south. Also the place to see *Primula scotica* and ther coastal wild flowers (27km, 17mi, 30min from Kirkwall or 10km, 6.5mi, 12min from Stromness).

. Skaill Loch is a good place to see overwintering waterfowl. In spring the south facing banks are covered with Primroses and other wild flowers. Waders and Arctic Terns nest nearby.

. Bay of Skaill This lovely beach is exposed to the northwest and changes greatly from year to year. At low tide there are extensive sands.

Skara Brae (*opening hours, admission charge, joint icketing with Skaill House, Tel 01856 841815*) is considered by many to be the Jewel in the Crown of Orkney's archaeology. Visitor Centre with audio-visual programme, museum and a replica of hut 7. On the way note the date tablets. Skara Brae has convenient viewing places with interpretation pan-ls. Hut 7 cannot currently be seen because the glass oof is grassed over. (400m walk from the Visitor Centre, about 8km (5mi) from Brodgar).

Skaill House (*opening hours, admission charge, joint icketing with Skara Brae*) is adjacent, and is the only uch house in Orkney open to the public (300m rom Skara Brae, 60min).

. Skeabrae & Twatt Airfields are both beside the A967 between the B9057 and Twatt. Several build-ngs remain, including the control tower at Twatt as well as the runways.

5. The Loons RSPB Hide Continue northwest on the B9055, bear right onto the A967 to Twatt, urn left at the old church for the Loons Hide. Waterfowl, waders, raptors and passerines may all be seen (5.5km, 3.5mi north of Skaill).

5. Marwick Head & Bay Turn right onto the B9056 and follow the sign for Marwick Head. Walk up the track to the Kitchener Memorial to see the huge seabird colony on the cliffs and Gannets offshore (2.5km, 1.5mi, 30min).

7. Barony Watermill (*opening hours, admission charge*) is on the Boardhouse Burn. This 19th cen-tury watermill is still in regular use.

8. The Palace as the village is called, has the gaunt remains of the 16th century Earl's Palace and the fine

St Magnus Kirk nearby. The excellent Birsay Bay Tearoom has superb views and a superlative salad bar with homegrown treats.

9. Brough of Birsay (*open at all times, admission charge when manned*) Tidal island reached by causeway and a fine sandy beach famous for *Groatie Buckies*. Norse era ruins, Romanesque church, longhouses and other buildings, plus replica Pictish symbol stone. Puffins on the cliffs in summer.

10. Skipi Geo & Whalebone A very satisfying 1km walk around the shore to this scenic inlet and unusual Blue Whalebone memorial.

11. Kirbuster Farm Musem (*opening hours, free admission*) is an 18th century "firehouse" and steading at the east end of Boardhouse Loch.

12. Durkadale RSPB Reserve is on the side road that runs to the south of Hundland Loch. Raptors, including Hen Harriers, Merlins and Short-eared Owls may be seen (3km, 2mi, 60min walk).

13. Costa Hill & Head is a good viewpoint. Walk up the track from a locked gate above Swannay Loch (3km, 2mi, 60min).

14. Burgar Hill & Lowrie's Water Birdhide Turn right off the A966 to the signposted hide at Lowrie's Water on Burgar Hill to see Red-throated Divers (2km, 1.5mi, 30min).

15. Broch of Gurness (*open at all times, admission charge when manned*) signposted off the A966 after Evie Village to Aikerness to visit the broch and its small museum. This is the best Iron Age site in Orkney and should not be missed (200m, 60min).

The Sands of Aikerness overlook Eynhallow Sound and are backed by extensive, but quarried out dunes. Knowe of Stenso is another ruined broch at the west end of the beach.

16. Click Mill (*open at all times*) is a Norse type ver-tical axis watermill in working order. Off the B9057 Hillside Road (1km walk, 30min).

17. Orkney Brewery (*opening hours*) at Quoyloo is a state of the art micro brewery with a visitor centre, cafe and shop. 3km (2mi) north of Skara Brae in the old Quoyloo School.

18. Corrigall Farm Museum (*opening hours, no charge*) is a late 19th century farm. Typical of Victorian period with working barn, grain kiln, horse-drawn machinery and livestock (1,000m from A986, 30-60min).

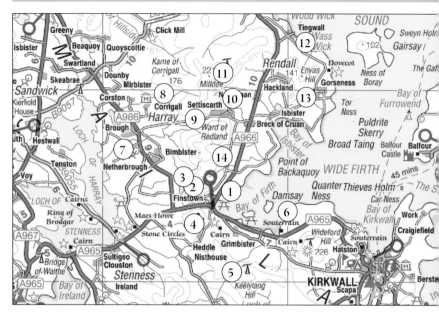

WEST MAINLAND The parishes of Harray, Rendall and Firth do not have the dramatic coastlines of the west side. Instead, they are the heartland of Orkney farming. The lochs, moors and sheltered coasts are havens for wildlife. There are several interesting archaeological sites to visit as well as many viewpoints and fine walks.

Finstown and Dounby have shops Post Offices. Dounby also has fuel pumps. The Merkister Ho on the shores of Harray Lc and the Smithfield in Dour are recommended eating plac Harray Loch is world famous a deservedly popular for its Bro Trout angling.

HARRAY, RENDALL & FIRTH

HARRAY

ARCHAEOLOGY

Burrian Broch
Hinatuin Stone
Knowe o' Burrian
Knowes o' Smirrus
Knowes o' Trotty
Netherbrough
Russland Broch

OLD FARMING

Corrigall Farm Museum
Winksetter
Bimbister
Click Mill

VIEWPOINTS & WALKS

Chair o' the Lyde
Lochside Viewpoint
Russland Drovers' Road
St Michael's Kirk
Stoneyhill Road

NATURE & WILDLIFE

Burn o' Rush
Harray Road End Reserve
Loch of Wasdale
Muckle Eskadale
Syradale

CRAFTS & SERVICES

Dounby
Fursbreck Pottery

RENDALL

Cottascarth Reserve
Doocot
Knowe o' Dishero
Loch of Brockan
Lyde Road
Mossetter Farmstead
St Thomas' Kirk
Tingwall
Wasswick WWII Battery

FIRTH

Binscarth Plantations
Burness Broch
Chapel Knowe
Cuween Cairn
Damsay
Finstown
Finstown Broch
Heddle Viewpoint
Holm of Grimbister
Ingashowe Broch
Keelylang
Loch of Wasdale
Redland Broch
Redland Road
Rennibister Earthhouse
Rennibister Neolithic
Stonehall Settlement
The Ouse

ORDNANCE SURVEY 1:50,000 AND 1:25,000 MAPS

OS Landranger Map 6	Orkney - Mainland
OS Explorer Map 463	Orkney - West Mainland

---

4. HARRAY, RENDALL & FIRTH (PAGES 39-41)

Suggested drives, bicycle rides and walks in the east of the West Mainland.

1. Finstown is equidistant from Kirkwall and Stromness (11km, 7mi, 15min).

2. Binscarth Plantations Park in Finstown and follow the signposted footpath to the woods, which are particularly bonny in spring when the Bluebells are in bloom.

3. Wasdale Walk If time permits continue along the Binscarth footpath to the Refuge Corner via Wasdale Loch. It is not recommended to return via the main road (6km, 4mi, 90min return).

4. Heddle Hill From the centre of the village take the steep hill up past the church. Scan the trees and bushes for passerines on the way. Opposite a large quarry there is a fine viewpoint over the Bay of Firth and North Isles.

Cuween Chambered Cairn Continue past the quarry and turn left onto a track to this fine Maeshowe-type cairn. Return to the carpark by one of the paths (3km, 2mi, 60min). The cairn can also be accessed from a signed carpark 1,000m east of the village.

5. Keelylang (221m) is reached by a track from Cruan, off the Old Finstown Road. Head for the TV masts for a stunning panorama. Short-eared Owls, Hen Harriers, Merlins and other species may be seen, as well as various species of waders. (5km, 3mi, 60min). Peat tracks can be followed to return via the Germiston and Heddle Roads.

6. Rennibister Earthhouse is signposted off the A965. It is a souterrain, and was probably the underground cellar of an Iron Age roundhouse (200m walk, 30min).

7. Netherbrough & Russland The side roads in this area east of Harray Loch offer many tranquil strolls, broch mounds to explore and fine views over the loch. The Merkister Hotel is a convenient lunch or dinner stop (up to 6km, 4mi, 60min).

The Harray Potter Andrew Appleby makes and sells pottery at Fursbreck Pottery. They also run courses and have self-catering accommodation. On the A986 near the Netherbrough Road.

8. Corrigall Farm Museum (*opening hours, no charge*) is a late 19th century farm, complete with animals and many artefacts. It is typical of the Victorian period and has a working barn, grain kiln, horse-drawn machinery and livestock (1,000m from A986, 30-60min).

9. Lyde Road goes from the A986 in Harray to A966 in Firth. This quiet road passes farmland before reaching the Chair o'the Lyde. (6km, 4mi, 15min).

The Knowes of Trotty are a series of mounds which form a Bronze Age cemetery. They are a short walk from the Lyde Road at Huntscarth. They can also be accessed from the Howe Road by following a track past Winksetter (1,000m, 60min).

10. Cottasgarth RSPB Reserve is at the east end of the Lyde Road. Well known for its Hen Harriers and other raptors, a brand new bird hide was opened here in 2015 (2km, 1.5mi, 60min).

11. Milldoe & Fibla Fiold (224m) has a transmitter mast and is accessed by a rough track, starting opposite the side road to Tingwall. It offers panoramic views over the Wide Firth, fine bird watching and solitude (8km, 5mi, 2h return).

12. Tingwall is the ferry terminal for Rousay, Egilsay & Wyre. It has a large broch mound and fine views over the North Isles.

13. Gorseness Road The side road running from Tingwall to Norseman offers lovely views of Gairsay. There are several interesting bays, including Hinderayre and Puldrite. The Loch of Brockan and Oyce of Isbister are haunts of wildfowl and waders (8km, 5mi, 30min).

Doocot At the Hall of Rendall, a 17th century Dovecot was renovated a few years ago. From here, paths and tracks can be followed around the shore and inland to explore this quiet corner.

14. Redland Road To take this side road turn off the Lyde Road after about 1,000m. There are fine views all along here. Peat tracks lead into the hill at several points (4km, 2.5mi, 15min).

Finstown Ouse is a large tidal basin north of the village. A paths runs round it, Common Seals, Otters, waterfowl, waders and Herons may be seen here (1.5km, 1mi, 30min).

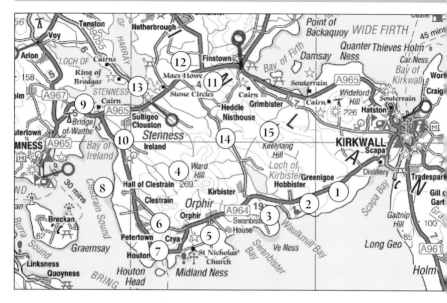

WEST MAINLAND The parishes of Orphir and Stenness are separated by the spine of the Orphir Hills. Both parishes have much to offer, with a varied selection of archaeological and historical sites ranging from the Neolithic Age to the 20th century.

Orphir forms the north shore of Scapa Flow, which dominates the view. There are fine beaches at Waulkmill Bay and Swanbister as well as many military relics. There is no shop, but it has the Noust Bar for bar meals.

Stenness, in contrast, is mostly land locked. It is named for the presence of so many of Orkney's magnificent Neolithic monuments. The Standing Stones Hotel and Stenness Shop provide meals and supplies, while Jerry's Ice Cream Parlour is a must if you love ice cream, highly recommended by many locals.

Nature There are also some of Orkney's best sites for observing wildlife, including birds, wild flowers, insects and mammals. These include moorland, lochs, wetlands, saltmarshes and the coast of Scapa Flow.

ORPHIR & STENNESS

ORPHIR	STENNESS	STENNESS
Bay of Houton	Barnhouse Stone	Maeshowe
Earl's Bu	Barnhouse Village	Millquoy Viewpoint
Greenigoe Viewpoint	Bigswell	Ness of Brodgar
Hall of Clestrain	Brig o' Waithe	Odinstone (site of)
Hobbister RSPB Reserve	Brodgar RSPB Reserve	Ring of Brodgar
Loch of Kirbister	Clouston Viewpoint	Standing Stones
Midland Hill Viewpoint	Comet Stone	Stoneyhill Road
Military sites, Houton	Cummi Howe Broch	The Bush
Orkneyinga Saga Centre	Dyke o' Sean	Tormiston Mill & Burn
Scorrabrae Viewpoint	Happy Valley	Unstan Chambered Cairn
St Nicholas Round Kirk	Loch of Harray	Watchstone
Ward Hill of Orphir	Loch of Stenness	
Waulkmill Bay	Lochside Viewpoint	

ORDNANCE SURVEY 1:50,000 AND 1:25,000 MAPS

OS Landranger Map 6	Orkney - Mainland
OS Explorer Map 463	Orkney - West Mainland

---

5. Orphir & Stenness (pages 20-31; 36-37)

Routes here assume starting from Kirkwall, but it can be joined at any point. Maeshowe and the Standing Stones can also be included.

1. Greenigoe Viewpoint There are fine views over Scapa Flow from the A964 near Greenigoe which take in the HMS *Royal Oak* wreck buoy, the Churchill barriers and Flotta. From Hobbister Brae the vista extends to Hoy and the Orphir Hills (6km, 4mi, 10min).

2. Hobbister RSPB Reserve Park in the signposted carpark and explore this *"magical mixture of land and sea, from sea cliffs to saltmarsh, from moorland to sandflats."* Hen Harriers, Short-eared Owls and Red-throated Divers may be seen. Peregrines nest nearby and could dramatically announce their presence. A gentle moorland, clifftop and beach walk (4km, 2.5mi, 60min).

3. Waulkmill Bay Park near the toilets and take the path down to the shore. The flat sandy beach ebbs dry, while the sheltered, low cliffs harbour many wild flowers. Otters may be seen around the burn (2km, 1.5mi, 60min).

4. Ward Hill of Orphir is the highest summit on the Mainland. It can be reached by a track about 500m west of the Orphir Kirk. A very satisfying walk in every season with a stunning panoramic view at the top (3km, 2mi, 60min). This walk can be extended by following the summit ridge to Bigswell. Peat tracks also go to Scorradale and the Stenness Hill.

5. Orphir Round Kirk (*open at all times, no charge*) is a 12th century church. Nearby are remains of a Norse farm (32km, 20min, 30min).

6. Scorradale Shortly before Houton, branch right up into Scorradale. Park at the top. Paths go south to Midland Hill with its viewpoint made famous by Thom Kent in 1919 (158m, 600m), and north to Gruf Hill (189m) and the Ward Hill.

7. Houton is the ferry terminal for Lyness and Flotta. In WWI there was a major seaplane base here, while in WWII it was very busy with craft serving the fleet. A short walk around the bay and up to the Head of Houton will reveal a fine vista of Scapa Flow (3km, 2mi, 60min).

8. Hall of Clestrain John Rae, who worked for many years for Hudson's Bay Company, was born at the Hall of Clestrain. It can be accessed via a short path from the A964 (1km, 0.6mi, 20min).

9. Brig o' Waithe Stop in the carpark west of the Bridge, where Stenness Loch drains into the sea. Herons, Common Seals, saltmarsh plants, waders and wildfowl may be seen; Otters are often present here (200m, 30min).

Unstan Chambered Cairn (*p38, free entry*) is situated off the A965 near the Brig of Waithe. The cairn is similar to the Tomb of the Eagles in South Ronaldsay and should be visited if there is not time to reach the latter. This tomb is a hybrid type with stalls in the chamber and a side cell (400m walk, 30min).

10. Clouston Road This narrow lane goes over Clouston Hill to the Stenness School. There are lovely views over Hoy Sound, Stromness as well as the Lochs of Stenness and Harray (3km, 2mi, 15min).

11. Happy Valley & Bigswell Now a community maintained woodland and garden. Created by Edwin Harrold, this little gem is an oasis of peace. It is perhaps best in spring with Bluebells, Daffodils and Primroses (400m, 60min).

12. Maeshowe (*opening hours, admission charge, booking required, 01856 761606*) should be visited if not already done. Other visits can be timed to suit (400m walk, 60min). Tours start from the Visitor Centre in Stenness Village, where there is an interesting book and gift shop.

The Standing Stones of Stenness (*open at all times, no charge*) are best in early morning or evening light. Nearby, the **Watchstone** stands sentinel over the landscape. The **Odinstone** stood between it and the Standing Stones.

Barnhouse Village (*open at all times, no charge*)is about 300m along a path leading towards the Loch of Stenness. The footings of several buildings are marked out. **Barnhouse Stone** can be best seen from the side road to Stenness Kirk.

13. Germiston Road goes from the A965 east of Maeshowe to the A964 near Waulkmill, with good birdwatching opportunities along the way. It passes close to Kirbister Loch (8km, 5mi, 20min).

14. Keelylang (221m) and the Hill of Lyradale can be reached from peat tracks going into the hill from Nisthouse or Kebro (6km, 4mi, 90min).

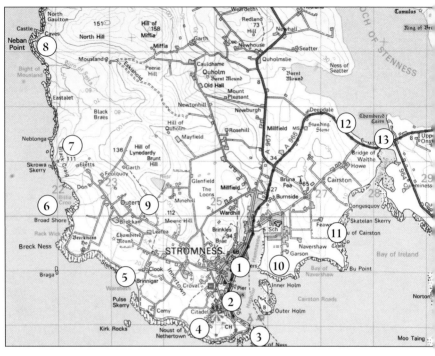

Stromness

Town

Login's Well
Pier Arts Centre
Stromness Museum
The Cannon
The Harbour

West

Black Craig
EMEC at Billia Cru
Neban Point
Ness Battery
North Gaulton Castle
Point of Ness
Warebeth Beach

East

Brig o'Waithe
Broch of Navershaw
Bu of Cairston Castle
Copland's Dock
The Holms
Deepdale standing stone

Viewpoints

Battery viewpoint
Black Craig
Brinkie's Brae

STROMNESS nestles along the east slopes of Brinkie's Brae, sheltered from the west and north. The town faces its excellent natural harbour, *Hamnavoe*, with the Hoy Hills and Scapa Flow in the background. There is much here for the visitor, from the highly acclaimed Pier Arts Centre and Stromness Museum to the events of Stromness Shopping Week.

Street The long, narrow and winding main street make this a walking town. It is best to park the car for the day, either on Ferry Road or at the Old Academy. Many of the shoreside houses are built with their gable ends facing the sea and have their own piers. The town is especially attractive from the ferry whist arriving or leaving.

Shops include Argo's Bakery and Stromness Coop for groceries; Quernstone for knitwear and gifts; Waterfront Gallery hol⌐ regular exhibitions and stocks ⌐ wide selection of gifts. Stromne⌐ Books & Prints is the smallest ar⌐ best bookshop in Orkney; near⌐ Northlight Gallery exhibits ta⌐ estries and other artwork.

Wishart's is an excellent "o⌐ fashioned" hardware shop, wh⌐ Sinclair's has everything for t⌐ angler; the Rope Centre is t⌐ place for anything nautical. Flet⌐ is a wonderful butcher which se⌐ prime Orkney beef at its be⌐ They also stock fine vegetables⌐ well as really good sausages a⌐ burgers.

Hotels and Restaurants ne⌐ the Pier Head, include the Fer⌐ Inn, Stromness Hotel and t⌐ Royal Hotel. Julia's Cafe and t⌐ Stromness Cafe are both nea⌐ by. Up the street, Hamnav⌐ Restaurant is for those seeking⌐ real "Taste of Orkney."

ORDNANCE SURVEY 1:50,000 AND 1:25,000 MAPS	
OS Landranger Map 6	Orkney - Mainland
OS Explorer Map 463	Orkney - West Mainland
Nicholson Maps	Kirkwall & Stromness Street guide

6. Stromness (pages 42-43)

Stromness is ideal for short walking or cycling exploration. The winding streets, narrow closes, varied coastline and interesting hinterland all beckon.

1. Stromness Town Centre & Harbour With all the activity of boats, the harbour is always a pleasant place to spend some time. The winding single main street has a variety of names, but is mostly just called "The Street".

The Pier Arts Centre (*opening hours, no charge*) in Victoria Street is an essential visit, with its permanent collection and regular exhibitions.

2. Stromness Museum (*opening hours, admission charge*) is in Alfred Street, south of the Lighthouse Pier (600m from Pier Head).

Brinkie's Brae (94m) overlooks the town. It can be reached by a path off Back Road. It is about 1,000m from the Pier Head and offers fine panoramic views.

Login's Well, in South End, is about 100m south of the Museum. Now sealed up, it formerly provided much of the town as well as visiting ships with water.

The Cannon is from a US privateer, captured in 1813. It is a pleasant place to sit and watch boats, birds and people coming and going.

3. Point of Ness is about 1,200m from the Pier head and is occupied by the Sailing Club, Golf Club and Camping Site.

The Citadel overlooks the Point of Ness and Hoy Sound. It was the site of a WWII gun battery, and is reached by a path from Back Road.

4. Ness Battery (*opening hours, admission charge*) was a major coast defence gun battery in both WWI and WWII. It has been cleaned up and renovated and is now open for guided tours. A side road from the Golf Club goes round the shore to the entrance (750m from Point of Ness).

5. Warebeth is an exposed sandy beach facing Hoy Sound and the Atlantic. It can be reached by a coastal path from the battery (1,500m), or by the side road going to Innertown.

6. Billia Crue Round the coast from Warebeth, this is the site used by EMEC for testing and developing devices intended to generate electricity using wave energy.

7. Black Craig (111m) is the most southerly of the West Mainland cliffs. It is accessed by a path from a carpark beside a ruined house called Fletts at the end of the Outertown Road.

8. Neban Point & North Gaulton Castle is about 2,400m north of the Black Craig. It is an easy walk along coastal heath. Several geos and waterfalls add interest to the route. North Gaulton Castle is a smaller version of the Old Man of Hoy, which can be seen to the south.

9. Stromness Backroads Inland, to the north of the town, there is a network of lanes, tracks and paths which is well worth exploring on foot or by bicycle. They can be accessed from the hillside road and from Back Road (up to 8km, 5mi, 2h).

10. Garson & Copland's Dock A path follows the shore from near the new Primary School to the site of the former Copland's Dock. There are fine views over Stromness from here. The Orkney Islands Council has built a large new pier and harbour area here (1,200m from the Pier Head).

11. Cairston The low shore can be followed all the way to the Brig o' Waithe, passing several interesting archaeological sites on the way (about 8km, 5mi, 90min return to Pier Head).

The Holms can be reached at low tide from Copland's Dock over slippery seaweed covered rocks. Care needs to be taken not to get stranded.

12. Deepdale Standing Stone is above an old quarry on the A965 facing the Loch of Stenness, about 1,000m northwest of the Brig o' Waithe.

13. Brig o'Waithe Stop at the carpark at the Bridge, where Stenness Loch drains into the sea. Heron, Common Seals, saltmarsh plants, waders and wildfowl may be seen and possibly an Otter early or late in the day (200m, 30min).

Unstan Chambered Cairn (*open at all times, no charge*) is situated off the A965 near the Brig of Waithe. The cairn is similar to the Tomb of the Eagles in South Ronaldsay and should be visited if there is not time to reach the latter. This tomb is a hybrid type with stalls in the chamber and a side cell (400m walk, 30min).

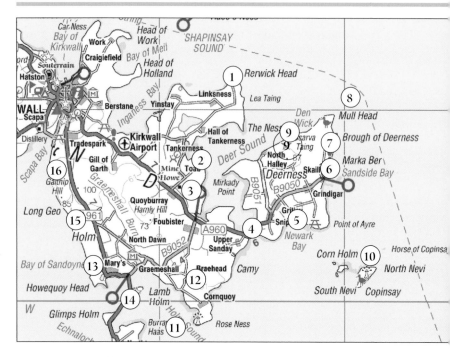

EAST MAINLAND The parishes of Tankerness, Deerness and Holm present a different face of Orkney. This quiet corner of Orkney was transformed by WWII, with the building of the Churchill Barriers, Netherbutton Radar Station, Grimsette Airport, numerous Coast Gun Batteries and many other military installations. The remains of most of these wartime defences may be visited today.

Services There is small country shop and Post Office in Deerness as well as shop and Post Office in Holm. The East Mainland is essentially an outdoors place to visit and lacks opportunities for intensive retail therapy apart from Shiela Fleet Jewellery in Tankerness.

Nature Short-eared Owls and Hen Harriers are common. There are numerous excellent places to view breeding waders and sea ducks. Wintering Great-northern Divers, Long-tailed Ducks and other waterfowl can be observed just offshore from a number of vantage points.

EAST MAINLAND

TANKERNESS

Bay of Suckquoy
Deer Sound
Kirkwall Airport
Loch of Tankerness
Mill Sand
Mine Howe
Rerwick Head
St Peter's Pool

DEERNESS

Brough of Deerness
Copinsay
Covenanter's Memorial
Dingieshowe
Mull Head
Newark Bay
Point of Ayre
Sandside Bay
St Peter's Pool
The Gloup

HOLM

Bay of Sandoyne
Castle Howe
Churchill Barriers
Graemeshall Loch
Holm Sound
Loch of Ayre
Netherbutton
Old St Nicholas Kirk
Paplay
Roseness
St Mary's Village
Wester Sand
WWII gun battery

LAMB HOLM

Blockship *Lycia*
Italian Chapel
Remains of Camp 60
WWII gun batteries

ORDNANCE SURVEY 1:50,000 AND 1:25,000 MAPS

| OS Landranger Map 6 | Orkney - Mainland |
| OS Explorer Map 461 | Orkney - East Mainland |

---

7. East Mainland (pages 52-53)

The East Mainland may lack the spectacular sea-scapes and archaeology of the West, but is attractive in a different, gentler manner. There are many lovely beaches, pleasant walks and prime birdwatching places to visit.

1. Rerwick Head was the site of coastal defence batteries in WWI and WWII. This is a prime bird-watching site in winter and the start of a fine coastal walk along the east side of Tankerness. The cliffs give way to lovely sands below Ness. Return along side roads from Hall of Tankerness Pier (10km walk, 14km, 9mi, 20min from Kirkwall).

2. Mill Sands Turn left at an old mill and park near the shore. The sands ebb dry, making this a very good place to see waders (up to 2km walk, 5km, 3mi, 10min from Rerwick Head).

Sheila Fleet Jewellery Workshop(*opening hours, no charge, but much temptation!*) is signposted next to an old church opposite the Sands.

3. Minehowe (open *by arrangement only*) is part of an Iron Age site, near Tankerness Community Hall, signposted off the A960 (3km, 2mi from Mill Sands.

4. St Peter's Pool The Bay of Suckquoy and St Peter's Pool are both prime wader spots, especially during migration times. Parking at both ends close to the shore (6km, 4mi from Minehowe).

Dingieshowe is the beach on the south side of the Deerness isthmus. There is a substantial broch mound and a fine sandy beach. From here a marked footpath goes along the coast to Barns of Ayre (8km, 5mi, 2h). Return along side roads.

5. Newark Bay on the south coast of Deerness has a small pier and a lovely stretch of sand. Park at the pier or at the east end.

6. Sandside Bay is on the east side of Deerness. This fine beach is backed by the remnants of sand dunes and remains a fine place for a walk and to search for wildflowers (2km, 1.3mi, 60min).

The Gloup is a large chasm formed by the collapse of a long cave. Park at the Mull Head carpark, near the small Visitor Centre (*open at all times, no charge*). The Gloup is about 100m along the path to the Mull Head.

7. Brough of Deerness This large rock stack can be accessed from the Mull Head path by the surefooted. There are ruined Norse buildings, including a church (1km, 0.6mi, 30min).

8. Mull Head (48m) is a further 1,000m around low but spectacular cliffs with fine views to Auskerry and Copinsay. The path continues back to the carpark (total walk 5km, 3.2mi, 2h).

9. Covenanters' Memorial overlooks Scarva Taing. It can be included on the Mull Head Walk (extra 3km, 2mi, 60min). A signposted road route goes from near the shop (2km walk).

10. Copinsay is a delightful small island southeast of Deerness which can be visited by boat. Newark Bay Pier is a convenient launching point. VisitOrkney should be consulted for operators.

11. Holm Sound is blocked by the Churchill Barriers. There are fine beaches at Howes Wick and Cornquoy as well as several good viewpoints over the South Isles and Scapa Flow. Follow the A960 and then the B9052 to Graemeshall (8km, 5mi, 15min).

12. Paplay The fertile southeast corner of Holm has a network of small lanes and small scale coastal attractions.

Graemeshall Battery is one of the best preserved and makes an interesting visit.

13. St Mary's Loch is on the west side of St Mary's Village, while Graemeshall Loch is to the east of the B9052. Both are prime birdwatching sites.

14. The Italian Chapel (*opening hours, no charge*) on Lamb Holm was built in WWII by Italian prisoners of war. It is an essential visit, not to be missed on any account. Turn left onto Churchill Barrier No1 at the junction with the A961.

Churchill Barriers From the Italian Chapel continue south on the A961. In winter look out for seaducks, and in summer breeding terns.

15. Netherbutton is about 4km, 2.5mi north of St Mary's on the A961. This was the location of a major WWII radar station. Many of the associated concrete buildings remain.

16. Return to Kirkwall on the A961. There are fine views over Scapa Flow overlooking Gaitnip Hill and Deepdale (5km, 3mi, 10min).

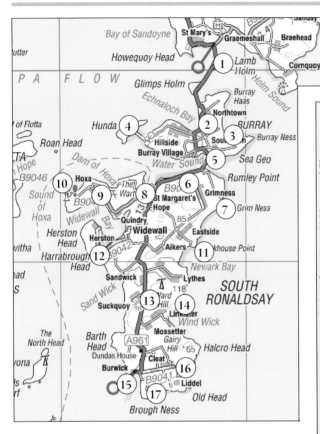

OVER THE BARRIERS South Ronaldsay and Burray have much to offer the visitor, including prime archaeological sites, bracing coastal walks and much of historical interest. There are also good opportunities for bird watchers, wild flower hunters and those seeking sea mammals.

Churchill Barriers The building of the Churchill Barriers in WWII transformed the islands socially and economically into part of the East Mainland. That said, there is a different feel to the place compared with the rest of Orkney, being only 10km (6mi) from Caithness.

"Ower the Barriers" To many, South Ronaldsay will be their arrival point in Orkney. The island's five "essential" visits could be described as *"stones, skulls, wool, colour, and highly satisfied diners"*. Any trip *"Ower the Barriers"* can include a range of new experiences, for a first time visitor or local person alike.

Beaches South Ronaldsay and Burray have many fine beaches. These include those at Barriers No 3 and No 4, The Bu Sands, Eastside and the Sand o'Wright.

Weather The Barriers can be dangerous in severe weather when breaking seas occur, especially on No2 Barrier. The roads are occasionally closed around high tide during storms.

ORDNANCE SURVEY 1:50,000 AND 1:25,000 MAPS	
OS Landranger Map 6	Orkney - Mainland
OS Landranger Map 7	Orkney - Southern Isles
OS Explorer Map 461	Orkney - East Mainland

8. OVER THE CHURCHILL BARRIERS (PAGES 54-57)

A journey across the Barriers, starting at one of Orkney's most visited gems, and ending it with a fine dinner. It takes in a wide range of different things.

1. The Italian Chapel (*opening hours, no charge*) on Lamb Holm was built in WWII by Italian prisoners of war. It is an essential visit, not to be missed on any account. Turn left onto Churchill Barrier No1 at the junction with the A961.

Churchill Barriers From the Italian Chapel continue south on the A961. In winter look out for seaducks, and in summer breeding terns.

Glimps Holm has a lovely sheltered beach facing Weddell Sound and Burray. There is a fine view from the summit (200m walk, 32m).

Burray Viewpoint There is a fine panorama from a large layby on the main road near Northtown.

2. Orkney Fossil & Vintage Centre (*opening hours, admission charge, shop, cafe*) has galleries on geology, fossils and minerals, the building of the Churchill Barriers and old Orkney trades. **Echnaloch** (page 96) is separated from Echnaloch Bay by a storm beach. This loch is always busy with waterfowl, easily observed from the car.

3. Old St Lawrence Kirk, at the southeast end of Burray, is an interesting roofless church.

Bu Sands stretches over a mile along the east coast. The South Links has beautiful wild flowers in summer.

4. Hunda is joined to the west end of Burray by a drying reef, over which a barrier was built in WWII. (4km, 2.5mi, 60min walk).

5. Ayre of Cara & Water Sound Huge quantities of sand have accumulated on the east side of Barrier No 4 to form a huge beach and dune system. The blockships have now been buried.

6. Orkney Marine-Life Aquarium (*opening hours, no charge, aquarium, shop*) has displays of live marine animals and also sells systems to ongrow baby lobsters in schools. offices and homes.

7. Grimness A fine circular walk from Honeysgeo (4km, 2.5mi, 60min).

8. St Margaret's Hope is a pretty little village and ferry port. There are several shops, the Craft Workshop, hotels and the Creel Restaurant.

9. Sand o' Wright is 2.5km west of the village on the B9043. This south facing beach is the venue of the Boys' Ploughing Match.

10. Hoxa Tapestry Gallery (*opening hours, no charge, shop, gallery, workshop*) Leila Thomson weaves her unique and wonderful tapestries here.

Hoxa Head overlooks the southern approaches to Scapa Flow. There are remains of gun batteries from WWI and WWII (park at the end of road, 5km, 3mi on B9043 from St Margaret's Hope).

11. Eastside St Peter's Kirk overlooks the Pool of Cletts and Newark Bay. There are fine walks both to north and south (3km, 2mi, from St Margaret's Hope War Memorial).

12. Harrabrough Head & Herston Park at the head of the Oyce of Herston for a fine walk around Herston. The Altar is a strange rock formation on Harrabrough Head. The pretty village of Herston faces Widewall Bay (4km, 2.5mi, 60min).

13. Olad Brae viewpoint has panoramic views of the Pentland Firth, Hoy and Scapa Flow (6km, 4mi south of St Margaret's Hope on A961).

Ward Hill Radar Site can be reached by a track near the viewpoint carpark (3km. 2mi walk).

14. Windwick is an exposed bay on the east side. There are fine coastal walks in both directions from the carpark (2km, 1.5mi from Olad Brae).

15. Burwick is the terminal for the summer passenger ferry to John o'Groats and the start of a coastal walk that extends up the west side of South Ronaldsay (up to 12km, 7.5mi, 3h).

16. Tomb of the Eagles (*opening hours, admission charge*) Along with its museum, this is one of the most impressive chambered cairns in Orkney. (3km, 2mi, on B9041 from Burwick).

17. Skerries Bistro and Tomb of the Otters (*opening hours, seasonal*) serves lunches and evening meals with fresh local fish and shellfish as specialities.

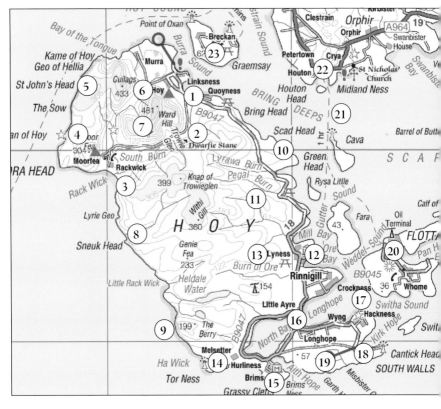

Hoy and Flotta can be reached by passenger ferry from Stromness to Moaness in the north or roro car ferry from Houton to Lyness in the south. The island is too big to fit in everything between first and la ferry. Booking is essential to ta a car.

Hoy

Hoy (North End)
Berrie Dale
Braebuster Broch
Chapel & Cemetery, Bu
Cuilags
Dwarfie Stone
Greenhill Broch, Whaness
North Hoy Nature Reserve
Old Man of Hoy
Rackwick
St John's Head
The Witter
Ward Hill
Whaness Burn

West Coast
Candle of the Sneuk
Ha Wick
Heldale Water

Hoglinns Water
Little Rackwick
Lyrie Geo
Mel Fea
Melberry& Sands Geo
Summer of Hoy
The Berry
Torness

North Walls
Aith Hope
Betty Corrigall's Grave
Binga Fea Viewpoint
Brims
Chapel of Brims
Duncan's Geo Chambered Cairn
Lifeboat Museum
Lyness Naval Cemetery
Lyness

Lyrawa Burn and Bay
Lyrawa Hill viewpoint
Melsetter House
North Bay
Pegal Burn and Bay
Scad Head
Scapa Flow Visitor Centre
The Skeo Broch
Water of Hoy
Wee Fea viewpoint

South Walls
Cantick Head Lighthouse
Green Hill of Hestigeo
Hackness Martello Tower
Hill o' White Hammars Reserve
Longhope
Osmondwall Cemetery
Outer Green Hill Cairn

9. Hoy & Scapa Flow (pages 58-61)

There is far too much to do in one day on Hoy, so it is best to visit the north or south, rather than rush round everywhere between ferries. There are great opportunities for walkers, and taxis can be prebooked to meet arrivals or departures. There is one shop in Longhope as well as three hotels. Lyness Visitor Centre has a cafe and there is another at Moaness.

. Moaness is convenient for visiting the north of Hoy. It is just possible to do the full tour between ferries. Nearby, to the north, the Sands of Klibreck face Burra Sound and Graemsay.

. Dwarfie Stone This unusual rock-cut tomb is 00m from the Rackwick Road along a boardwalk. It nestles under the Dwarfie Hammars.

. Rackwick is a beautiful beach facing the Atlantic. It is flanked by 150m cliffs and hemmed in by high ills (8km, 5mi from Moaness).

. Old Man of Hoy (137m) This famous rock stack is reached by a path from Rackwick (5km, 3mi from Rackwick).

. St John's Head is a steep climb north from the Old Man. There are dizzy views from this 351m headland (3km, 2mi).

. Cuilags (433m) is on the route back to Moaness from St John's Head (2km, 1.25mi). Return to the road at Sandy Loch.

. Ward Hill of Hoy (479m) is a steep climb from andy Loch (2km, 1.25mi). Another route starts from the Dwarfie Stone carpark.

. The Sneuk (190m) The West Coast Walk from Rackwick to Melsetter passes this dramatic headland at the Summer of Hoy (12km, 8mi).

. The Berry (170m) overlooks Tor Ness and the Green Heads (4km, 2.5mi from Melsetter).

0. Scad Head faces Houton across the Bring Deeps and has a WWII gun battery (2km walk). yrawa Hill AA battery overlooks Scad Head (9km, .5mi from Lyness).

1. Pegal Burn is the largest in Orkney. It has a pretty valley and estuary.

2. Lyness was a major naval base in WWI and WWII. The Scapa Flow Visitor Centre, (*opening ours, no charge*) next to the ferry terminal, tells the story of the base with many exhibits, indoor and outdoor. Lyness War Cemetery is nearby.

13. Wee Fea Viewpoint (130m) overlooks Longhope. The Naval HQ building here has an excellent view of Scapa Flow. there are huge oil tanks within the hill (2km, 1.5mi from Lyness).

14. Melsetter House (*visits by arrangement only Tel 01856 791352*).

15. Longhope Lifeboat Museum (*opening hours, to view Tel 01856 701332*) has the former lifeboat *Thomas McCunn* as its main exhibit. Off the B9047 at Brims.

16. Longhope was the scene of much activity during wartime, serving the fleet and many army bases. Today it has a little harbour, where the lifeboat is based, a shop and a hotel.

17. Hackness Martello Tower & Battery (*opening hours, admission charge*) was built during the Napoleonic Wars to protect assembling convoys. The site has been extensively refurbished and has a large gun (18km, 11mi from Lyness).

18. Osmondwall Cemetery, Kirk Hope has the poignant memorial to the crew of the Longhope Lifeboat lost in 1969.

Cantick Head Lighthouse was first lit in 1858 and has fine views over the Pentland Firth.

19. Hill of WhiteHammars Reserve is noted for having *Primula scotica* on maritime heath above the attractive low cliffs.

20. Flotta makes a very interesting visit, with several coast defence batteries, Stanger Head Naval Signal Station and a small Visitor Centre, as well as the Oil Terminal.

21. WWI German High Seas Fleet was moored around Cava. Seven large ships remain there and are dived on by many enthusiasts every year.

22. Houton is the ferry terminal for sevices to Lyness and Flotta (Kirkwall 18km, 11mi, 30min, Stromness (14km, 9mi).

23. Oxan Point, Graemesay WWII Coast Defence battery next to Hoy Low Lighthouse. It can be seen from the Stromness to Moaness ferry, which also calls at Graemesay Pier.

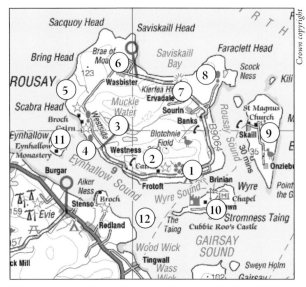

Crown copyright

ROUSAY, EGILSAY & WYRE are easy to reach from the West Mainland. If time is short there is no better place to start island bagging in Orkney than Rousay. A circular tour of the island is a pleasant 21km (13mi). Three islands in one day is quite possible by careful study of the ferry timetable. In reality there is so much to see and do that several days are necessary.

Services Rousay offers many services to the visitor. These include shops, restaurants, bars and t services. Minibus tours are available, as well as hotel and other accommodation. The island off a great of variety of things to and do. Egilsay and Wyre have facilites for visitors.

Archaeology is prominent including Neolithic, Iron Age Norse, Medieval and more recent sites. The Neolithic chambered cairns, Iron Age brochs and Viking era sites are spectacular. Perhaps the most essential place to visit for those interested the *Orkneyinga Saga* tales is Magnus Kirk on Egilsay.

Nature The islands are all in Natural Heritage, with t RSPB Reserves, and large are designated as Sites of Spec Scientific Interest. All of Orkney moorland birds can be observed here. In winter the sounds home to overwintering seadu and divers.

The maritime heath on the west coast and moorland of the interior are home to many species of wild flowers. It would be easy to spe a whole day just searching for t rare orchid. Much of Egilsay traditionally managed to attract the elusive Corncrake, mak it a haven for wild flowers a breeding waders.

.

Transport The ferry runs several times per day from Tingwall Rendall and offers plenty of ti on each island. For Rousay car needs advance booking, would not be needed on Egil or Wyre. All are ideally sui for cycling. Occasional excursi are organised to Eynhallow. T ferry terminal at Tingwall is ab 21km (13mi) from Kirkwall Stromness, and well served buses from both.

ROUSAY, EGILSAY & WYRE

ROUSAY

Bigland Round Cairn
Blackhammer Cairn
Blotchnie Field viewpoint
Brough Farm
Digro Memorial
Faraclett Head Walk
Green Gairsty
Interpretation Centre
Kierfea summit viewpoint
Knowe of Burrian, Broch
Knowe of Hunclett, Broch
Knowe of Swandro
Knowe of Yarso Cairn
Leean Viewpoint
Loch of Scockness
Midhowe Broch
Midhowe Cairn
Moaness
Muckle Water
Napier Commission
Quandale Viewpoint
Rinyo
Saviskaill Bay
Scabra Head

St Mary's Kirk
Taversoe Tuick Cairn
The Wirk
Tofts Farmhouse
Trumland House (Gardens)
Trumland RSPB Reserve
Wasbister
Westness House (private)
Westness Walk
Yetnasteen

EGILSAY

St Magnus Kirk
St Magnus Cenotaph
Onziebust RSPB Reserve

WYRE

Cubbie Roo's Castle
St Mary's Kirk
The Taing

EYNHALLOW

Monastery

ORDNANCE SURVEY 1:50,000 AND 1:25,000 MAPS

OS Landranger Map 6   Orkney - Mainland
OS Explorer Map 464   Orkney - Westray, Papa Westray, Rousay

10. Rousay, Egilsay & Wyre (pages 64-65)

Heritage Centre At the ferry terminal on Brinian *er* (*open at all times, no charge*).

The Circular Tour 21km (13mi) can be done *etween* ferries by car or bicycle. If sites of interest *re* visited and detours made; allow a whole day.

rumland RSPB Reserve (*open at all times, no *arge*) Long and short walks starting near Taversoe *uick* (1.5-5km, 1-3mi).

rumland House Gardens (*opening hours, admis-on charge*) are being restored to their former glory.

aversoe Tuick Chambered Cairn is just west of *rumland* House above the B9064. Unusually, it is *uilt* on two levels.

Blackhammar Chambered Cairn is built on a *ne* viewpoint just above the road (2.5km, 1.5mi *est* from the pier on the B9064).

nowe of Yarso Chambered Cairn is about 400m *p* a track from Frotoft. Two more lie nearby, the *nowes* of Ramsay and Lairo, but are ruinous.

Muckle Water & Peerie Water are reached by *rough* hill road from Westness. Paths and peat *acks* can be followed through the centre of the *land* to Wasbister and Sourin.

Westness Walk starts from the carpark above *Midhowe* and follows a marked trail through a *ariety* of archaeological sites with fine views over *ynallow* Sound (4km, 2.5mi, 2h walk, 8km, 5mi *om* the pier).

Midhowe Chambered Cairn is enclosed within a *rge* steel building. This impressive stalled cairn is *ne* largest in Orkney.

Midhowe Broch is the best preserved of a row of at *ast* five facing a similar row along the Evie shore. *Vith* its outbuildings and ramparts it is second only *o* the Broch of Gurness.

t Mary's Kirk is roofless, and fell out of use in *820, but remains standing today.

The Wirk is nearby. This square tower is part of an *nexcavated* 13th century hall.

rough Farm ruins date from the 18th century and *ave* been uninhabited since 1845.

Scabra Head & Quandal About 800m after the *Midhowe* carpark, a dramatic viewpoint opens up *ver* Quandal and Eynhallow Sound. The coastal *cenery* and clifftop maritime heath here is full of *nterest* to the naturalist.

6. Wasbister in the far northwest of Rousay (4km, 2.5mi from Quandal viewpoint, 10km, 6mi return to pier clockwise).

Saviskaill Bay has a small sandy beach, Nousty Sand. The bay extends for 5km (3mi) to Faraclett Head in the east.

7. The Leean Viewpoint is on the B9064 east of Wasbister. Park at a disused quarry. There is an expansive vista over the Westray Firth.

Kierfea (235m) is a brisk 400m climb. From here the view extends over Saviskaill Bay and all the way round to Sourin and Egilsay beyond.

Sourin Brae This steep hill offers fine views over Rousay Sound and Egilsay.

Digro is about 500m from the top of the hill on the south side. A plaque commemorates the eviction of James Leonard.

8. Faraclett Head Walk starts near the farm and proceeds around this headland, passing impressive cliffs and several ancient sites (3km walk).

Yetnasteen overlooks the Loch of Scockness, from where it takes an annual drink.

9. Egilsay can be reached by the ferry *"Eynhallow"*. This attractive small island has an interesting history.

St Magnus Kirk is the site of the murder of Earl Magnus in c.1117. Its distinctive round tower is visible from all around (800m from the pier).

St Magnus Cenotaph is about 500m from the church and commemorates the saint.

Onziebust RSPB Reserve covers a large part of Egilsay and is farmed very successfully for the benefit of wildlife.

10. Wyre is the small island just south of Rousay and is also reached by the ferry.

Cubbie Roo's Castle dates from the 12th century. It is about 1,100m from the pier.

St Mary's Kirk is just to the east and is also 12th century.

The Taing is the most westerly point on Wyre, and a prime spot for seals and birds (about 3km from the pier).

11. Eynhallow Monastery is Norse and about 600m from the beach.

12. Wyre Sound offers good birdwatching oppor-tunities, especially in winter.

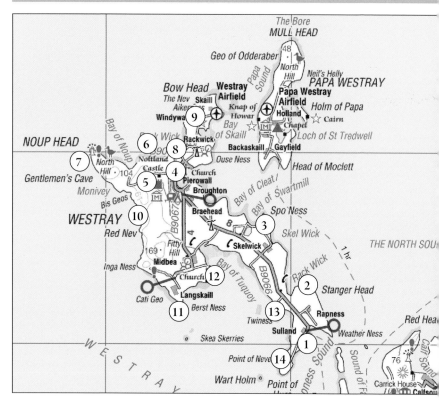

Westray, often referred to as "The Queen of the Isles", is the second largest of the North Isles. In many ways it could be referred to as "Orkney in Miniature". The island has dramatic cliffs, good beaches and ancient sites. The Brough of Burrian near Rapness is the best place in Orkney to see Puffins without too much effort.

Westray Services The island h plenty of services for the visit These include hotels, B&Bs a self-catering accommodation, well as cafes. The local shops Aladdin's caves, full of all mann of goods essential for island li as well as interesting items visitors to buy.

Westray Craft Trail includ a wide variety of products sale, including knitwear, te tiles, Orkney Chairs, paintin photography, pottery and oth crafts.

Transport There are daily ro vehicle ferry and air services fro Kirkwall. There is also a reg lar passenger boat service fro Pierowall to Papay. Island tou bicycle hire and a local bus serv are all available.

Westray

Aikerness Walk	Loch of Saintear
Bay o' Tafts	Loch of Swartmill
Bay of Kirbist	Mae Sand
Bay of Tuquoy	Noltland Castle
Castle o' Burrian (Puffin)	Noup Head Lighthouse
Cott Chambered Cairn	Noup Head RSPB Reserve
Cross Kirk	Pierowall
Faray & Holm of Faray	Queena Howe Broch
Fitty Hill (169m) highest hill	Quoygrew Norse site
Gentlemen's Cave	St Mary's Kirk
Gill Sands	Stanger Head (Puffin)
Grobust Beach	Swartmill Bay
Holm of Aikerness	The Ouse
Knowe o' Skea	Tuquoy Walk
Knowe o' Burristae Broch	West Coast Walk
Links of Noltland	Westray Airfield
Loch of Burness	Westray Heritage Centre

ORDNANCE SURVEY 1:50,000 AND 1:25,000 MAPS	
OS Landranger Map 5	Orkney - Northern Isles
OS Explorer Map 464	Orkney - Westray, Papa Westray, Rousay

11. Westray (pages 66-69)

Rapness Ferry Terminal The ferry from Kirkwall docks at Rapness. If taking a car, booking is essential (30km, 19mi, 95min).

Castle o' Burrian is signposted 2km north of Rapness. This rock stack and surrounding banks is the best place to see Puffins in Orkney (1,000 walk from old mill, 60min).

Stanger Head is about 700m further on and well worth visiting for seabirds, wild flowers and the view.

Swartmill Bay is a beautiful small sandy beach facing Papay. It is backed by Swartmill loch and marshland (7km, 4.5mi from Rapness).

Pierowall is the only village on Westray. It nestles around a fine harbour and has the hotel and shops (11km, 7mi from Rapness).

Westray Heritage Centre, (*opening hours, admission charge*) is an excellent start to any visit, with fixed and seasonal displays, the Pierowall Stone and, when in residence, the *"Westray Wife"*.

St Mary's Kirk is mostly 16th century but is built on a much more ancient chapel site.

Sand o' Gill is revealed at low tide at the north end of the bay. It is very popular with waders.

Lochs of Burness & Saintear to the west and south of Pierowall, respectively, are home to many waterfowl and waders.

Noltland Castle was built in the 16th century. This gaunt shell is 1,000m west of Pierowall.

Grobust is perhaps the most beautiful beach in Westray, if not Orkney. This north facing bay is backed by constantly shifting sand dunes and machair (1,500m from Pierowall by various routes).

Queena Howe is a ruined broch mound at the west end of Grobust Beach.

Links of Noltland Eroding sand dunes have revealed extensive Neolithic structures. these are currently being investigated.

North Coast Walk A delightful coastal walk from Grobust to Pierowall via Rackwick.

Quoygrew Norse House) lies above the shore on the northeast side of Rackwick. (Grobust to Pierowall via Rackwick 5km, 3mi, 90min).

Noup Head RSPB Reserve The west cliffs go 8km (5mi) from here to Inga Ness. The Noup holds a huge colony of seabirds in summer, including an increasing colony of Gannets (6km, 4mi, west of Pierowall, the last 2km is on a rough track).

Noup Head Lighthouse marks the northwestern point of Orkney. There are fine panoramic views from this headland.

Gentlemen's Cave is one of several large caves on this coast. Access is only possible with local knowledge and suitable equipment.

8. Rackwick is a rocky bay on which, in winter, vast quantities of seaweed (ware) builds up after northerly storms.

9. Aikerness Walk The northernmost tip of Westray has the airfield and a low, but interesting, coastline. It includes sandy beaches, saltmarsh, maritime heath and low cliffs (12km, 7.5mi walk).

10. West Coast Walk This goes from Kirbest to Noup Head along the clifftops (9km, 6mi, 4h, this is a linear walk, transport needed for return).

Fitty Hill (169m) is 1,000m from the southern end of the West Coast Walk. It should be climbed on the way for its panoramic views.

11. Knowe o' Burrastae is a large broch mound which is slowly being eroded by the sea (600m from the end of the B9067, 8km, 5mi from Pierowall).

Mae Sand is below Langskaill. This 600m expanse of white sand is backed by a large area of dunes and machair.

Berst Ness has extensive remains of a prehistoric settlement.

Knowe o' Skea is a prominent mound on the southern tip of Berst Ness which was recently excavated to reveal an Iron Age site.

12. Ness of Tuquoy Walk Park below Tuquoy and follow the coast past Cross Kirk to Mae Sand. Return via the road, 6km (4mi) walk, (6.5km, 4mi south of Pierowall on B9067).

Cross Kirk is a 12th century Norse church.

13. Bay of Tafts is an attractive southwest facing beach near the ferry terminal.

14. Rapness Walk & Beaches The low cliffs between Stanger Head and Weatherness (2.5km, 1.5mi) make a good extension to a Puffin visit. The south end has several fine beaches and walks to explore while waiting on the ferry.

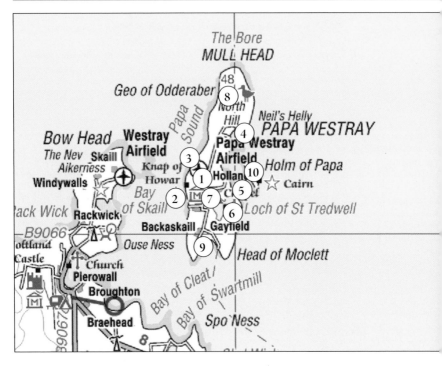

PAPAY or **PAPA WESTRAY** lies to the northeast of Westray. This little island is a delight to visit, whether for archaeology, birds, wild flowers, beautiful coastline or just for peace and quiet. There is no daily roro car ferry, but there are daily return flights from Kirkwall, and a passenger ferry from Pierowall.

Knap of Howar Many will head straight for the Knap of Howar, the oldest standing house in Orkney, before visiting St Boniface Kirk and the beautiful beaches at North and South Wick. The Knap of Howar alone merits a trip here. The nearby St Boniface Kirk is more recent, but also interesting.

Nature Naturalists will spend an enjoyable day exploring the North Hill Reserve, with its extensive maritime heath. Primula scotica thrives here along with other maritime flora. Arctic Terns a Arctic Skuas breed here, while t small bird cliff at Fowl Craig busy with Guillemots, Razorb and Kittiwakes in summer.

The island is infamous in ornith logical history as the site of t killing of the last British Gr Auk, in 1813. St Tredwell's Lc and surrounding marsh ha waterfowl and waders. Today, t is one of the best places to list for the elusive Concrake, wh breeds here, but is rarely seen.

Transport A daily passeng ferry runs from Pierowall Westray. There are two sa ings per week from Kirkw one of which also goes to Noi Ronaldsay. Loganair also flies Papay two or three times da There are special Excursion fa which are available only to p sengers staying for a minimum one night.

ORDNANCE SURVEY 1:50,000 AND 1:25,000 MAPS

OS Landranger Map 5   Orkney - Northern Isles
OS Explorer Map 464   Orkney - Westray, Papa Westray, Rousay

12. PAPAY (PAGES 70-71)

Papay has much to offer the visitor. Three short walking tours are suggested here, which take in the whole island. A full circuit would take a long day and really needs at least an overnight stay.

Papay Airfield is conveniently situated for visitors in the middle of the island. Several walks are suggested, including a 16km (10mi) circumnavigation of the coast.

. CENTRAL LOOP - head south from the airport towards Holland Farm, 8km, 5mi, 2-3h.

. Knap of Howar is on the west coast, about 2,000m southwest of the airfield. These houses date from c.3600BC and are an essential visit.

. St Boniface Kirk is about 1,000m north of the Knap of Howar. This restored 12th century church remains in use. There is a Norse hog-backed gravestone in the kirkyard.

Munkerhouse is the local name of nearby ruins, suggesting a monastic pesence here.

. North Wick From St Boniface take the road east and then north up the island for approx 2,000m. The road ends at North Wick.

Cott, at the south end of the bay was one of the main places for pulling up boats.

. South Wick has several areas of fine sand between rocky sections. It is sheltered by the Holm of Papa, and is the site of the Sooth Pier.

The Old Pier was used by the steamers before the Moclett Pier was built.

Nouster has several well preserved nousts, where boats were pulled up and sheltered.

Hookin Mill is on the shore east of St Tredwell's Loch. Its undershot waterwheel was not very effective.

. St Tredwell's Loch is much frequented by waterfowl and waders.

St Tredwell's Chapel is in a small peninsula projecting into the east side of the loch. It is built on an Iron Age broch.

. Holland Farm has a fine 19th century and a 17th century house. A bothy has been made into a small folk museum. Return to the airport, after stocking up with a picnic from the shop.

8. THE NORTH HILL - head north from the airfield to the RSPB Reserve. Total walk is about 10km (6mi).

North Hill RSPB Reserve has varied habitats, including maritime heath, small lochs, marsh and low cliffs. The best time to visit is early summer (circuit 6km, 4mi, 2h).

Fowl Craig is 1,000m along the east coast from Hundland. Despite its diminutive size, this bird cliff offers very good closeup views of breeding seabirds in summer.

9. SOUTH END OF PAPAY CIRCUIT From the shop take the road to the South Pier, then follow the coast all the way to the Head of Moclett, return via Vestness and Backaskaill (circuit 8km, 5mi, 2h).

6. St Tredwell's Loch is much frequented by waterfowl and waders.

St Tredwell's Chapel is in a small peninsula projecting into the east side of the loch. It is built on an Iron Age broch.

Head of Moclett has low cliffs with a natural arch and a sandy beach on the west side.

Bay of Moclett is sheltered from west and east. It has a fine sandy beach with links behind.

Broch of Bothican was to the east of Moclett Pier, but is usually covered in sand.

Minister's Flag is a large flat stone on the Vestness beach, where the minister used to land from Westray.

Backaskaill Burnt Mound is just south of the road. Nearby springs would have fed its trough.

10. HOLM OF PAPAY is the small island sheltering South Wick, and is about 700m from the Old Pier. It can be accessed by boat. The island is about 1,000m long and has three chambered cairns.

North Cairn is a delapidated Orkney-Cromarty type stalled cairn.

Diss o' the Holm, or the South cairn is a very large Maeshowe-type with a 20m chamber.

Bay of South Cruive is a small sheltered sandy beach famous for its Groatie Buckies. The broken rocks of the Holm of Papay storm beaches are favourite nesting places for Storm Petrels (*Mooties*) and Black Guillemots (*Tysties*).

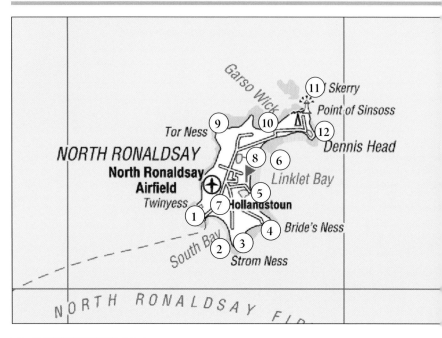

NORTH RONALDSAY

Airfield - established 1968
Bird Observatory - south end
Bride's Ness - old chapel site
Broch of Burrian - Iron Age
Cruesbreck farm mound
Dennis Head
Dennis Loch
Dennis Rost
East Indiamen losses
Golf Course - nine holes
Holland House - 18th century
Hooking Loch
Howmae Brae - Iron Age site
Kirnest
Linklet Bay
New Lighthouse - built 1854
North Ronaldsay Sheep
North Ronaldsay Trust
Old Beacon - built 1789
Old Kirk - built in early 1800s
Seal Skerry - Seals
Sheep Dyke - 19km long
South Bay
Strom Ness
The Stan Steen
Treb Dykes (Muckle Gairsty)

NORTH RONALDSAY is the most northerly island in Orkney. Its relative isolation and lack of a daily ferry give it a special character. It is easy to reach by a daily air service from Kirkwall.

The island is the home of the North Ronaldsay Sheep. They are kept outside the Sheep Dyke that surrounds the island for most of the year. This small, hardy breed thrives on a diet of seaweed. The Dyke was built in the 1830s and is 19km (12mi) long.

The Old Beacon at Dennis Head was one of four lighthouses erected in Scotland in the late 1780s, and first lit in 1789. The low-lying islands of North Ronaldsay and Sanday had for centuries been a dangerous graveyard for ships, especially in foggy weather.

Accommodation here includes a guest house, B&B and self catering. Meals and refreshments are available at the Bird Observatory, pub and at the Lighthouse Cafe.

Supplies are available at the sho Tours and taxis can be booke Bicycles are also available to hi and fuel is on sale.

Locally Produced Wool Yar and knitwear is on sale on th island. The Yarn Company wor shop is at the lighthouse and ca be visited.

Bird Observatory Mar visit North Ronaldsay Bir Observatory during the migratic seasons. A large number and va iety of species pass through ann ally. Visitors can take part in bi watching, ringing and learn abo our avian visitors.

Transport Getting to Nor Ronaldsay is easy by Logana from Kirkwall Airport. Tho staying one night or more g a discounted air fare. Advan booking is essential. There is weekly ferry (twice in summe but this is subject to delays d to weather. In summer there a occasional day trips.

ORDNANCE SURVEY 1:50,000 AND 1:25,000 MAPS

| OS Landranger Map 5 | Orkney - Northern Isles |
| OS Explorer Map 465 | Orkney - Sanday, Eday, N Ron, Stronsay |

13. NORTH RONALDSAY (PAGES 72-73)

Most visitors arrive at the airstrip near Holland House. Day excursion sailings from Kirkwall are laid on for a few Sundays in summer.

Sheep Dyke   This unique feature runs right around the island for 19km (12mi).

North Ronaldsay Sheep are kept outside the Sheep Dyke except at punding time when the clipping is done and the ewes and lambs separated.

1. North Ronaldsay Bird Observatory is at the soutwest end, just above the pier.

2. South Bay has a fine sandy beach backed by machair and dunes stretching about 1,500 from the pier to Strom Ness.
Howmae Brae, at the east side of South Bay, has Iron Age roundhouses buried in the sand. **Kirbist** is about 200m inland from Howmae and has associations with Viking saga tales.

3. Strom Ness is the most southerly point. It faces the often ferocious North Ronaldsay Firth and is the closest point to Sanday.
Broch of Burrian is an impressive Iron Age broch, surrounded by ramparts.

Reef Dyke is a dangerous skerry lying about 2km (1.5mi) east of Strom Ness, the graveyard to many a ship.

4. Bride's Ness is about 1,500m northeast of Stromness and the site of an ancient chapel.

5. Hooking Loch is surrounded by a small area of wetland and is good for waterbirds.

6. Linklet Bay extends for over 5km (3mi)

Brides Ness to Dennis Head. There are extensive stretches of sand with some dunes and machair, as well as rocky sections.

The Golf Course is near the middle of Linklet Bay and has 9 holes.

7. Holland House is still used by the local laird. Its gardens attract many migrant birds.
Stan Stane is about 700m north of the pier and has a small hole pierced through it.
Treb Dykes cross the island in two places dividing it into Northyard, Linklet and Southyard. They can be made out in several places.

8. Ancum Loch is easily observed from the road. It is popular with waders and waterfowl.

9. Tor Ness, the northwesternmost point has an exposed, rocky shore. There is a small sandy beach at Lens Wick and many skerries offshore.

10. Loch of Garso, in the northeast, almost splits the island in two. It is surrounded by marshy ground, attractive to waders and waterfowl.

11. Dennis Head Lighthouse is the tallest land-based lighthouse in the British Isles. Organised visits to the tower can be booked.

12. Dennis Head Old Beacon is on the easternmost tip of North Ronaldsay. It was built in 1789 and is one of Orkney's iconic symbols. (5.5km, 3.5mi, 75min from the pier).
Kirk Taing near the Beacon is the site of an ancient chapel.
Bewan Pier was built originally to transport material for the Old Beacon and remained the Lighthouse Pier for many years.

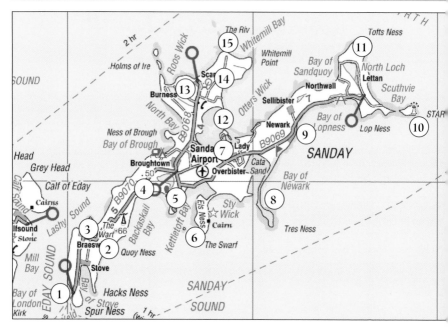

Sanday is the largest of the North Isles. It is very low lying, apart from the south end, and has many beautiful sandy beaches backed with machair. In summer there is a riot of wild flowers, while the shallow bays are a favourite with many migrant and resident wading birds.

Quoyness Chambered Cairn Although there are many sites of archaeological interest, only the Quoyness chambered cairn is actually on display to the public. This impressive Maeshowe-type cairn on the peninsula of Elsness dates from about 3000BC and very much merits a visit.

Scar Boat Burial In 1991, an exciting find at Scar was a Viking boat burial, in which three people were interred. A spectacular whalebone plaque was among the artefacts found. This may be seen along with other artefacts, at the Orkney Museum in Kirkwall.

Start Point Lighthouse is painted with vertical black stripes to distinguish it from North Ronaldsay lighthouse, which has red stripes. Start Island can be reached at low tide by crossing Ayre Sound.

Accommodation on Sanday includes hotels, guest houses, B&Bs and self catering establishments. Meals are available in several places, and there is a good selection of shops. Transport, tours, car hire and internet access are all available. Sanday is a great place to visit for a day, but to fully appreciate its many delights a stay of at least a couple of days is recommended.

Sanday	
Backaskaill Bay	Ortie
Bay of Lopness	Otterswick
Bay of Sandquoy	Pool Settlement Site
Black Rock	Quoyness Chambered Cairn
Cata Sand	Rethie Taing
Egmonds Howe Cairn	Roos Loch
Elsness	Sanday Golf Course
Farm Mounds	Scar
Gump of Spurness	Scuthvie Bay
Holms of Ire	Start Point Lighthouse
Kettletoft village	Stove 19th century farm
Lopness WWII Radar Station	Submerged Forest
Mount Maesry	The Wart (65m)
North Loch	Tres Ness
Old Cross Kirk	Wasso Broch
Old Lady Kirk	Whitemill Bay
Orkney Angora	WWI German destroyer B98

ORDNANCE SURVEY 1:50,000 AND 1:25,000 MAPS OF SANDAY

OS Landranger Map 5	Orkney - Northern Isles
OS Explorer Map 465	Orkney - Sanday, Eday, N Ron, Stronsay

---

14. Sanday (pages 76-77)

Sanday is deceptively large. Lady Village is about 13km (8mi) from Loth Ferry Terminal. From Lady Village to Kettletoft is about 5km (2mi), to Start Point about 10.5km (6.5mi) and to Whitemill Bay about 8km (5mi). A full tour is over 40km (25mi).

1. Loth Ferry Terminal is on the southwest extremity of Sanday, Spurness, opposite Eday. Journey times are: Kirkwall 95min; Eday 20min.

2. Stove is about 1.5km (1mi) north of Loth on the B9070. The ruined farm is interesting.

Doun Helzie The coastline east of Stove has attractive sandy bays with low cliffs and a natural arch.

3. The Wart (65m) is the highest point on Sanday and affords panoramic views.

Pool, at Laminess is the site of a large prehistoric settlement with Neolithic, Iron Age, Pictish and Norse buildings. There is nothing to see here, but there are artefacts in Orkney Museum.

4. Backaskaill Bay is a beautiful 2,000m sandy beach with dunes between Backaskaill and Kettletoft.

Bea Loch just north of Kettletoft, is the largest on the island. It often holds large numbers of waterfowl and waders.

Old Cross Kirk, roofless and situated above Backaskaill Bay, is 800m down a side road next to the farm of How.

5. Kettletoft is the former main harbour, with a shop and two hotels (12km, 7.5mi, from Loth).

The Ouse & Little Sea, the inner part of Kettletoft Bay, to the east of the village. The B9069 skirts the north shore and is ideal for birdwatching.

Old Lady Kirk, on the edge of the Little Sea is famous for its *"Devil's Scratch Marks"*.

6. Els Ness Turn right 100m east of Old Lady Kirk and park after 1,200m; many archaeological sites as well as the long beach at Quoy Ayre.

Quoyness is one of the finest Neolithic chambered cairns in Orkney. It is about 1,000m along a path from the Els Ness carpark.

7. Lady Village is the largest settlement with the Community Shop and Post Office (13km, 8mi, from Loth).

Sanday Airfield is between The School and Lady Village, in the centre of the island. Flights to Kirkwall take about 15 minutes.

Cata Sand is a large, flat, shallow and sandy bay. The east side is protected by a 3km (2mi) line of high sand dunes (1,500m east of Lady village).

Plain of Fidge was a dummy airfield in WWII and today the site of the Golf Course.

8. Tres Ness is an interesting walk. From the B9069 follow a track round the shore to Tres Ness farm with its old enginehouse, then onwards, passing Neolithic and Iron Age sites (9km, 5.5mi, 2h walk).

9. Lopness Bay stretches 4km (2.5mi) from Newark to Lopness. It is backed by high dunes, dune slacks and lochs.

RAF Whalehead was a Chain Home radar station in WWII. Some of the the buildings remain as well as of the nearby backup at Lettan.

Scuthvie Bay is another lovely long sandy beach, with dunes and machair behind.

10. Start Point Lighthouse is situated on Start Point, the most southerly tip of Sanday. It can be accessed at low tide across Ayre Sound (4km, 2.5mi walk from the end of the public road).

Mount Maesry A well-preserved Maeshowe-type chambered cairn near the lighthouse.

11. North Loch is an excellent birdwatching site to the north of Lopness.

Tofts Ness, northeast of North Loch has many cairns and other prehistoric remains.

12. Otterswick is a large, shallow bay surrounded by muddy beaches. The inner part, the Lamaness Firth, ebbs dry.

Black Rock is on the meeting point of all three parishes, 1,300m northwest of Lady.

Submerged Forest Ancient tree roots and branches lie under the sand at Otterswick.

13. Roos Loch is another excellent birdwatching site. A road and track go right round it.

Holms of Ire A trio of islands where Grey Seals pup in autumn, accessible at low tide only.

14. Scar is the site of a Viking boat burial. Artefacts may be seen in the Orkney Museum.

Orkney Angora at Breckan, near Scar has a fascinating shop and workshop.

15. Whitemill Bay is perhaps the finest beach in Orkney. It faces North Ronaldsay and is backed by beautiful links, (18km, 11mi, from Loth).

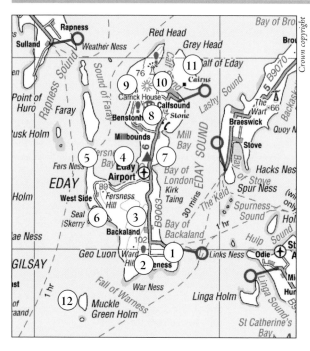

Chambered Cairns

There are many chambered cairns on the island, some in good condition and some ruinous. Vinquoy is a Maeshowe-type cairn which over looks Calf Sound. This interest ing structure has been repaired and is built of large sandstone blocks. It has two pairs of side cells and the main chamber is over 3m high inside.

Carrick House

was first built in 1633 for one of the Stewarts. In 1725 nearby Calf Sound was the scene of the capture by its then owner, James Fea, of "Pirate Gow" Gow and his fellow pirates were tried and hanged in London.

Wildlife

The hide on the Mill Loch is a very good place from which to observe Red-throated Divers, and other waterfowl which nest here. Whimbrels, Hen Harrier, Merlins, Arctic Skuas and Short-eared Owls may also be seen on the island during the summer. The many flat sandy beaches are excellent for waders.

Walks

Eday is fine walking coun try, with a number of marked routes. Leaflets describe these walks in detail. All of the beaches are easily accessible by tracks or paths. The moorland has many peat tracks which provide conven ient routes to the hilltops.

Facilities

Eday offers many ser vices to visitors, including guided tours, taxis, car hire and accom modation. Snacks, lunches and evening meals are available, while the Community Shop offers a wide range of supplies.

Transport

Orkney Ferries oper ate daily services from Kirkwall. There are also connections with Sanday and Stronsay which can allow all three islands to be explored without returning to Kirkwall.

Eday (ON *Eid-ey*, Isthmus Isle) is less fertile than the other outer North Isles and much of it is peaty heather moorland. Its cen tral position means that there are excellent views of much of Orkney from the top of the Ward Hill, or from the Red Head.

Stone of Setter is 4.5m high and very prominent overlooking Calf Sound and near the Mill Loch, in a focal point of the landscape. The weathered monolith is cov ered in lichen, and perhaps the most impressive standing stone in Orkney.

Eday

Bay of Greentoft	Mill Bay
Bay of London	Mill Loch
Braeside chambered cairn	North School
Calf of Eday	Noup Hill
Calf Sound	Paplayhouse
Carrick House	Red Head
Castle of Stacklebrae	Sands of Doomy
Church Chambered Cairn	Sands of Mussetter
Fersness	Stone of Setter
Flaughton Hill	Sui Generis
Green	Vinquoy Chambered Cairn
Heritage Walk	Vinquoy Hill
Huntersquoy Cham'd Cairn	Ward Hill
Loch of Doomy	Warness Walk
London Airport	Westside Walk

ORDNANCE SURVEY 1:50,000 AND 1:25,000 MAPS OF EDAY

OS Landranger Map 5	Orkney - Northern Isles
OS Explorer Map 465	Orkney - Sanday, Eday, N Ron, Stronsay

---

15. EDAY (PAGES 78-79)

Getting to Eday - daily by sea from Kirkwall, crossing time is 75min (25km, 16mi), by air from Kirkwall takes 11 minutes on Wednesdays only.

1. Backaland Pier is in the southeast corner of the island, about 8km (5mi) from the shop.

Roadside Pub overlooks the pier and is an ideal place to start or end your visit depending on which ferries are being taken.

2. Warness Walk encompasses the southwest corner of Eday, (3km, 2mi).

Green is the site of a Neolithic settlement. Near Veness, about 1,000m south of the pier.

Warness Burnt Mound is prominent about 1,000m west of the Greentoft road end.

Castle of Stacklebrae is at the east end of Greentoft Bay and may be a Norse castle.

Veness The name suggests the presence of an early chapel on this headland.

EMEC has the world's first tidal energy testing site in the Fall of Warness. Machines, ships and work-boats may be visible.

3. Flaughton Hill (99m) has the water reservoir and panoramic views of the North Isles. A track goes up from the B9063 about 2.5km (1.5mi) from the pier. A fine circular walk takes in Leeniedale and Ward Hill summits via peat tracks.

4. Sands of Mussetter & Sands of Doomy comprise the best beach on Eday. Backed by dunes and dune slacks they are attractive to birds and host lovely wild flowers in summer.

5. Fersness The large quarry above the shore is the traditional source of much of the stone for St Magnus Cathedral.

Fersness Bay Walk takes in several of the best bays on the island and encompasses a variety of habitats. Good for birds in all seasons and wild flowers in summer (8km, 5mi, 2h).

6. Sealskerry Bay & Westside This attractive cove faces south, sheltered from the west by Seal Skerry. Many seals do indeed haul out on the skerry and around the bay.

Westside Walk This is a concatenation of the Warness and Fersness Walks, and takes in the whole of the southern half of Eday (18km, 11mi, 4h, starting and ending at Backaland Pier).

7. Bay of London This small, muddy bay is very popular with waders and can be reached by several short tracks opposite the airfield.

London Airport is centrally located between Doomy Loch and London Bay.

Eday Heritage & Visitor Centre is in the old Baptist Chapel and is open daily. It has an exhibition area and cafe.

8. Eday Heritage Walk starts at the shop, passing Mill Loch, the Stone of Setter and several chambered cairns before reaching the viewpoint of Vinquuoy Hill (76m) (8km, 5mi, 3h).

Stone of Setter is the tallest (4.5m), and most impressive, standing stone in Orkney.

Fold of Setter is a Bronze Age enclosure for holding sheep or cattle.

Braeside & Huntersquoy are chambered cairns on the route of the Heritage walk.

Vinquoy Chambered Cairn has been restored and is on the south flank of the hill.

9. Vinquoy Hill Viewpoint (76m) offers a superb panoramic view over Calf Sound to the east and Westray to the northwest.

Red Head (70m) The northern tip of Eday has bright red sandstone cliffs. There are fine panoramic views from here, about 2,300m north of Vinquoy Hill and a fine extension to the walk.

Red House is a restored croft next to Paplayhouse on the west side of Vinquoy Hill.

10. Calf Sound lies between Eday and the Calf of Eday. It has a very strong tidal flow, and is the background of much historical drama.

Carrick House dates from 1633 and is situated in a superb position on Calf Sound. Visits by arrangement only, Tel 01857 622260.

Pirate Gow was famously captured in Calf Sound in 1725 by James Fea.

Stephen's Gate Walk is a fine coastal route on the east side of Calf Sound.

North School has interesting scholastic and nautical displays, including part of HMS *Otter*.

11. Calf of Eday hosts many breeding birds and has chambered cairns and a salt works.

12. Green Holms lie southwest of Eday and are a major breeding ground for Grey Seals.

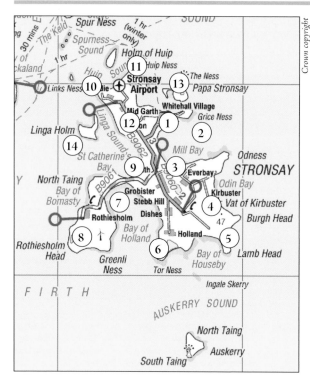

Archaeology There are a number of archaeological sites on the island, but none of great interest, no doubt because it has been intensively farmed for many years. There is a large chambered cairn at Kelsburgh near the Bu and two smaller ones at Lamb Head. A number of broch mounds are prominent on the coast.

Herring Stronsay was a major Herring fishing centre for centuries. The Dutch were fishing in Orkney waters in late Norse times and by the 17th century had over 2,000 boats working the North Sea. The island was used as a harbour for Dutch and Fife boats during the season for hundreds of years up until 1937, when the industry collapsed due to over fishing.

Whitehall Village was very busy during the fishing season and once boasted the longest bar in Scotland. On Sundays there were hundreds of boats tied up however, the increased catching power of the steam drifter meant that the stocks of Herring were exhausted before WWII. Today the harbour is home to a few inshore creel boats. The former Fishmarket has been done up as an interpretation centre, cafe and hostel.

Facilities Stronsay offers good but limited facilities to visitors being primarily an agricultural island. Accommodation, meals, car and bike hire are all available. There are several shops, and the story of the Herring fishing is told in the Old Fishmarket.

Transport Orkney Ferries operate daily services from Kirkwall. There are also connections with Eday and Stronsay which can allow all three islands to be explored without returning to Kirkwall.

STRONSAY is one of the most fertile islands in Orkney. It has a much indented coastline, with many very fine beaches, as well as low cliffs on the southeast side with several large caves, and a natural arch at the Vat of Kirbuster.

Although most of the island is agricultural land, the many fine beaches, several lochs and areas of wetland as well as the moorland of Rothiesholm, mean that there is a large variety of habitat and feeding areas for wildlife.

STRONSAY

Auskerry	Meikle Water
Ayre of Myres	Mill Sands and Mill Bay
Benni Cuml, Houseby	Moncur Memorial Church
Burgh Head	Odness
Earl's Knowe	Old Fishmarket
Golgotha monastery	Papa Stronsay
Greenhill, Huip	Rothiesholm aerogenerators
Grice Ness	Sand of Rotheisholm
Herring Fishing	St Catherine's Bay
Hillock of Baywest	St Nicholas Chapel site
Holm of Huip	St Peter's Chapel
Kelp Making	The Castle Bird Reserve
Kelsburgh Chambered Cairn	Vat of Kirbuster
Lamb Head	Well of Kildinguie
Linga Holm	Whitehall Village

ORDNANCE SURVEY 1:50,000 AND 1:25,000 MAPS OF ORKNEY

OS Landranger Map 5   Orkney - Northern Isles
OS Explorer Map 465   Orkney - Sanday, Eday, N Ron, Stronsay

16. STRONSAY (PAGES 80-81)

Getting to Stronsay - by sea from Kirkwall, daily, crossing time is 95min (32km, 20mi), flights from Kirkwall take 11 minutes .

1. Whitehall Village is the main settlement on Stronsay and owes its existence to the kelp making and Herring fishing industries.

Old Fishmarket The building where herring was formerly auctioned is now the heritage centre, as well as a hostel and cafe.

Sea-washed toilet This edifice stands at the west end of the village and is cleaned by the sea.

Athenia **Boathouse** *SS Athenia* was sunk off Ireland by U-30 in 1939. This boathouse is one of the ship's lifeboats that drifted ashore here.

2. Grice Ness, the peninsula east of Whitehall, has a chambered cairn, kelp pits, old piers, small sandy beaches and lochs with marshes.

Kelp-making lasted for over 100 years from 1721 and was a major industry on Stronsay.

St Peter's Chapel is a ruin in the old kirkyard 500m west of Whitehall on the coast.

3. Mill Bay stretches from Grice Ness to Odness on the east side. Mill Sands are about 2.5km (1.5mi) of beautiful sheltered beach.

Kildinguie is an ancient well and chapel site at the north end of Mill Sands, below Hunton. Kildinguie was famous for its curative power.

Moncur Memorial Church is a unique and interesting building, built in the 1950s, in memory of a former minister, James Moodie.

Bird Reserve is situated at The Castle and run by ornithologist and artist, John Holloway.

4. Walk, Odin Bay to Houseby This walk around the southeast of Stronsay has spectacular cliff scenery and archaeology (11km, 7mi, 3h).

Vat of Kirbuster is a large collapsed cave, or gloup, with a dramatic 20m-high natural arch (1,000m from carpark).

Burgh Head is the most easterly point on the island. The Brough is a stack with remains of walls on top, which may have been a monastic site.

5. Lamb Head has several interesting features, including the Dane's Pier, Whale Geo and Hells Mouth. There are also chambered cairns and a well-preserved broch.

6. Tor Ness Circular Walk starts from Holland Farm and follows the coastline to Tor Ness. Wild flowers, birds, seals, a chambered cairn and a broch are all features (8km, 5mi, 2h).

Mels Kirk is a small sandy bay where Common Seals may be observed from a hide.

Lea Shun Loch with a bird hide above the Sand of the Crook, northeast of Tor Ness.

Sand of the Crook 1,300m of golden sand running from Tor Ness to The Crook.

Ward of Houseby is a prominent chambered cairn facing the Bay of Houseby.

Benni Cuml (page 558) is a large broch mound above the shore, southwest of Houseby.

7. Sand of Rothiesholm is Stronsay's third large beautiful beach, stretching for 1,800m round the northwest side of the Bay of Holland. A waymarked walk takes in the beach and the north shore, facing St Catherine's Bay (6km, 4mi, 2h).

Hillock of Baywest is a large broch mound 300m inland from the Bight of Baywest.

Kelsburgh Chambered Cairn is a long mound near the shore at Ver Geo.

8. Rothiesholm, the large peninsula in the southwest of Stronsay is mostly heathland.

Latan, on the east side of Rothiesholm, has well defined remains from kelp-making.

9. St Catherine's Bay faces west and has a 1,000m stretch of lovely sand with links behind.

10. Links Ness is the northwest tip of Stronsay, and home to many Grey Seals during the pupping season in autumn.

11. Oyce of Huip is a large, shallow inlet, sheltered by Huip Ness that holds many waterfowl and waders during winter and migration times.

12. John's Hill Viewpoint at 43m is the highest point on Stronsay, about 3km (2mi) west of Whitehall.

13. Papa Stronsay shelters Whitehall Village from the north and east. Now home to the Golgotha Monastery, it has several antiquities.

14. Linga Holm, or the Holm of Midgarth, is a wildlife reserve, and a major Grey Seal breeding site in the autumn.

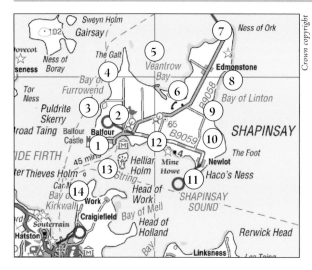

Crown copyright

Balfour Castle The house o Sound was built in 1674 b Arthur Buchanan, on the site o the present Balfour Castle. I 1775 Thomas Balfour marrie Frances Liginier, whose mone paid for the Sound Estate. Soo the island was transformed with new house, Cliffdale, the villag then called Shoreside, farm build ings and dykes all being built.

In 1846 David Balfour, who ha made a fortune in India, inherite the estate, which now included th whole island. He had the hous transformed into the presen building. It has not change much in 150 years, with most o the original furnishing and deco still in place. It is now run as " family country house hotel wit top class facilities and a worl class chef."

Visiting Shapinsay makes a ideal first island visit, which can b as short as the boat journey ther and back, a day trip or a "proper stay. As with every other part o Orkney, there is much to see an do. It would be very relaxing t stay for a week without ever leav ing the island.

Accommodation Shapinsa offers B&B and self-caterin accommodation as well as th exclusive Balfour Castle. Meal are available at the Smithy restau rant near the pier and at Hilto Farmhouse. Boat trips and guide tours are also a feature.

Transport Shapinsay has fre quent daily ferry links wit Kirkwall and is the easiest to reac of all the North Isles. It is an ide island to tour by bicycle, a circula tour being about 24km (15mi excluding detours. These ma include the nature reserves, beach es and walks to various points o interest.

Shapinsay is only 20 minutes from Kirkwall by roro ferry. It was one of the first areas where the old runrig system was changed to larger fields, and is nearly all cultivated today.

Broch of Burroughston The only archaeological site on display, having been excavated in 1862. It is surrounded by a ditch and rampart, and has a well preserved interior, nearly 3m high inside. There is an intact corbelled cell in the entrance passage and a large central well accessed by steps.

Mor Stane The 3m Mor Stane is of indeterminate date and is said to have been thrown by a giant from the Mainland at his departing wife. On the north side below Lairo Water, Odin's Stone may have been a Norse meeting place.

Norse Power Shapinsay featured in the unsuccessful bid by King Haakon of Norway to reassert Norse power in the west of Scotland in 1263. The great fleet was mustered here in Elwick Bay, before its departure for the Clyde.

Shapinsay

Balfour Castle	Old Kirk and Graveyard
Balfour Village	Orkney Stained Glass
Broch of Burroughston	Point of Dishan Douche
East Hill & East Craigs	Quholm
Elwick Mill	Salt Ness
Elwickbank viewpoint	Sandy Geo, Ness of Ork
Gas House	Skenstoft Beach
Haco's Ness (Hackness)	Smithy Heritage Centre
Holm of Burghlee	Smithy Restaurant
Howe Broch	Steiro Broch
Linton Chapel	The Gatehouse
Little Vasa Loch	The Ouse & Lairo Water
Mill Dam RSPB Reserve	Vasa Loch
Mor Stein	WWII Coastal Defence Battery
Odin Stone	

ORDNANCE SURVEY 1:50,000 AND 1:25,000 MAPS OF ORKNEY

OS Landranger Map 6	Orkney - Mainland
OS Explorer Map 461	Orkney - East Mainland

---

17. SHAPINSAY (PAGES 82-83)

Getting to Shapinsay The roro ferry "MV Shapinsay" operates frequent services from Kirkwall. The 7km (4.2mi) crossing takes 20 minutes.

1. Balfour Castle is prominently sited west of Balfour Village . It is a family country house hotel Tel 01856 771282.

Balfour Village was formerly known as Shoreside and overlooks Elwick Bay.

Elwick Bay is sheltered from the east and south by Helliar Holm.

2. Mill Dam RSPB Reserve has a hide from which breeding and visiting waterfowl and waders may be observed (1,500m from the pier).

3. Vasa Loch & Little Vasa Water are also prime sites for waterfowl and waders. Seaducks and divers may be seen offshore in winter (2km, 1.5mi from the Mill Dam).

Grukalty Pier is about 1,000m south of Vasa Loch. Along with Furrow of Agricola and Noust of Agricola, nearby, some say that this is evidence for a Roman visit.

4. Salt Ness has a WWII coast defence battery and anti aircraft gun site with fine views over the Wide Firth (5km, 3mi north of the pier).

5. Veantrow Bay is wide and north-facing, stretching from Galt Ness to the Ness of Ork.

The Ouse & Lairo Water lie behind Venatrow beach, Shapinsay's longest stretch of sand at over 2km (1.5mi). Several roads and tracks lead down to the shore from the B9058.

The Odin Stone is a large flat rock on the beach below Lairo Water.

Inskift of Skenstoft is the beautiful name of the east end of Veantrow Beach, accessed via the Skenstoft or Swartaquoy roads off the B9058.

6. Quholm is near the shore at Innsker, a beautiful little cove north of Girnigoe. It is the birthplace of William Irvine, the father of the American writer, Washington Irvine.

Washington Irvine was born in Manhattan in 1783, two of his best known works are, *"Rip van Winkle"* and *"Tales of the Alhambra"*.

7. Ness of Ork is the most northeasterly point on Shapinsay (11km, 7mi, from the pier).

Sandy Geo is a beautiful small cove facing the Stronsay Firth. A strong tide flows past here. *Groatie Buckies* may be found by the lucky.

The Hillock is a large broch mound which is being eroded by the sea on the south side of the geo.

Noust of Erraby is another "secret" sandy beach about 800m south of Sandy Geo.

8. Burroughston Broch is about 1,500m south of the Ness of Ork, with a carpark off the B9058. This large broch was excavated in 1862, left to decay, used as a quarry, then cleaned up and "restored", but remains an interesting visit.

9. Linton Chapel is a small ruin above the north shore of the Bay of Linton.

10. East Hill & East Craigs Walk is a nature reserve. A fine coastal path starts near Dog Geo at an old quarry and goes all the way to Haco's Ness, passing caves, geos and the Holm of Burghlee, a rock stack, on the way (4km, 3mi, 2h).

Castle Bloody is a chambered cairn covered by a mound about 1,300m east of the Mor Stein and not far from the"Fit' o' Shapinsay.

Mor Stein, a large standing stone stands on a small rise (36m) 800m inland from the B9059.

The Fit o' Shapinsay is at the midway point of the walk, where the coastline makes a sharp right turn. It is marked "The Foot" on maps.

11. Hacosness is also known as Hackness and is the most southerly point of Shapinsay. There is a chambered cairn on the southwest tip.

Bay of Sandgarth The beach here is also called the Pool of Haroldsgarth and is reckoned by Shapinsay folk to be the best on the island (8km, 5mi, from the pier).

12. Lady Kirk is now roofless and stands in the graveyard beside an older, ruined church.

Broch of Steiro is another broch mound on the coast below the graveyard.

13. Helliar Holm has a chambered cairn on its summit and a lighthouse on the south side. Access is only possible by boat.

14. Thieves Holm has many gruesome tales connected to it. The ferry passes this small island on its way to and from Kirkwall.

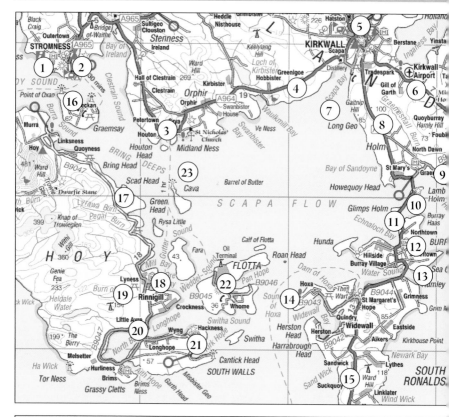

WORLD WAR I
PLACES TO VISIT

Kirkwall	Orkney Museum
St Ola	Carness Battery
	Caldale Camp
Orphir	Houton Base
	Upper Sower Battery
Birsay	Marwick Head
Stromness	Ness Battery
Holm	Clett Battery
Burray	Blockship *Reginald*
S Ronaldsay	Hoxa Head Battery
	Windwick
Hoy	Martello Towers
	Lyness
Cava	WWI Wrecks
Flotta	Innan Neb Battery
	Roan Head Battery
	Stanger Head Battery
	HMS Vanguard buoy
	Prudentia buoy

WORLD WAR II
SITES TO VISIT

Kirkwall	Orkney Museum
	Wireless Museum
	Black Building (site)
	Hatston airfield
St Ola	Carness Battery
	Grimsetter Airfield
	Scapa, oil tanks
Orphir	Houton Head
Rendall	Queenamuckle Battery
Birsay	Northside Radar
	Twatt Airfield
Sandwick	Yesnaby gun training
	Skeabrae Airfield
Stromness	Ness Battery
	Links Battery
Holm	Clett Battery
	Netherbutton Radar
	Graemeshall Battery
	Rockworks camp
Tankerness	Rerwick Head Battery
Deerness	AA battery site
	radar site

Lamb Holm	Italian Chapel
	Churchill Barriers
	Lamb Holm Battery
Burray	Northfield Battery
	Hunda Barrier
S Ronaldsay	Balfour, Hoxa Battery
	Ward Hill radar site
	Cara Battery
Hoy	Scad Head Battery
	Skerry Battery
	Scad Head AA Battery
	South Walls radar
	Lyness
Graemsay	Oxan Point Battery
Flotta	Buchanan Battery
	Stanger HeadBattery
	Gate Battery
	Innan Neb Battery
	Golta Battery
	Neb Battery
	Piers and Old Cinema
Fara	AA batteries
Sanday	Lopness Radar
Shapinsay	Castle Battery
	Galtness Battery

ORDNANCE SURVEY 1:50,000 AND 1:25,000 MAPS OF ORKNEY			
OS Landranger Map 6	Orkney - Mainland	OS Landranger Map 7	Orkney - Southern Isles
OS Explorer Map 462	Orkney - Hoy	OS Explorer Map 461	Orkney - East Mainland

18. Scapa Flow & Wartime Orkney

1. Ness Coastal Battery, Stromness (page 43, *opening hours, admission charge*) was a major coastal defence gun battery in both WWI and WWII (750m from Point of Ness along a side road).

2. The Cannon is from a US privateer, captured in 1813.

The Citadel overlooks the Point of Ness and Hoy Sound. It was the site of a WWII anti-aircraft battery, and is reached by a path from Back Road.

Stromness Museum (Page 42, *opening hours, admission charge*) is in Alfred Street, south of the Lighthouse Pier (600m from Pier Head).

3. Houton (page 46) In WWI this was a major seaplane base. There is a fine vista of Scapa Flow from here (14km, 8mi, 15min from Stromness).

4. Greenigoe Viewpoint offers fine views over Scapa Flow which take in the HMS *Royal Oak* wreck buoy (10km, 6mi, 10min).

5. Kirkwall (page 12) Hatston was a major Fleet Air Base in WWII and the now demolished "Black Building" the command station.

Orkney Wireless Museum (*opening hours, admission charge*) in Kirkwall has displays on wartime radar and communications.

6. Grimsetter Airport is 5km (3mi) to the east of Kirkwall on the A960. This was another WWII airbase, first RAF, then Fleet Air Arm.

Inganess Bay has the forward half of an oil tanker torpedoed in WWII.

7. Gaitnip Viewpoint there are fine views over Scapa Flow overlooking Gaitnip Hill and Deepdale (6km, 4mi, 10min on A961).

8. Netherbutton Radar Station is about 4km, 2.5mi north of St Mary's on the A961. This was the location of major WWII radar station. Many of the concrete buildings remain.

9. Holm Battery (page 48) was built after the sinking of HMS *Royal Oak* in 1939 (2km, 1.5mi east of St Mary's Village access by footpath).

10. The Italian Chapel (page 54, *opening hours, no charge*) on Lamb Holm was built in WWII by Italian prisoners of war. It is an essential visit, not to be missed on any account. Turn left onto Churchill Barrier No 1 at the junction with the A961.

11. Churchill Barriers (page 54) From the Italian Chapel continue south on the A961 across the Churchill Barriers. There are substantial remains of several blockships from WWI and WWII.

12. Burray (page 56) The Fossil & Vintage Centre has a display on the building of the Churchill Barriers. There is a coast defence battery on the northeast of the island (4km, 3mi from Chapel).

13. Ayre of Cara (page 56) Huge quantities of sand have accumulated on the east side of Barrier No 4 in the last 70 years.

14. Hoxa Head (page 56) overlooks the southern approaches to Scapa Flow. There are remains of gun batteries from WWI and WWII (park at the end of road, 5km, 3mi on B9043 from St Margaret's Hope).

15. Olad Brae (page 56) carpark has panoramic views of the Pentland Firth, Hoy and Scapa Flow (6km, 4mi south of St Margaret's Hope on A961).

Ward Hill Radar Site can be reached by a track near the viewpoint carpark (3km. 2mi walk).

16. Oxan Point, Graemsay (page 465) has a WWII coast defence battery next to Hoy Low Lighthouse. It can be seen from the Stromness to Moaness ferry.

17. Scad Head faces Houton across the Brig Deeps and has a WWII gun battery (2km walk). Lyrawa Hill AA battery overlooks Scad Head (9km, 5.5mi from Lyness).

18. Lyness (page 60) was a major naval base in WWI and WWII. The Scapa Flow Visitor Centre, next to the ferry terminal, tells the story of the base with many exhibits, indoor and outdoor. Lyness War Cemetery is nearby.

19. Wee Fea Viewpoint (page 60, 130m) overlooks Longhope. The Naval HQ building here has an excellent view of Scapa Flow (2km, 1.5mi from Lyness).

20. Longhope (page 60) was the scene of much activity during wartime, serving the fleet and many army bases.

21. Hackness Martello Tower & Battery (page 61) was built during the Napoleonic Wars to protect assembling convoys (18km, 11mi from Lyness).

22. Flotta makes a very interesting visit, with several coast defence batteries, Stanger Head Port Signalling and Observation Centre and a small Visitor Centre; ferry from Houton.

23. WWI German High Seas Fleet (page 46) was moored around Cava. Seven large sunken ships remain there which are of great interest to divers.

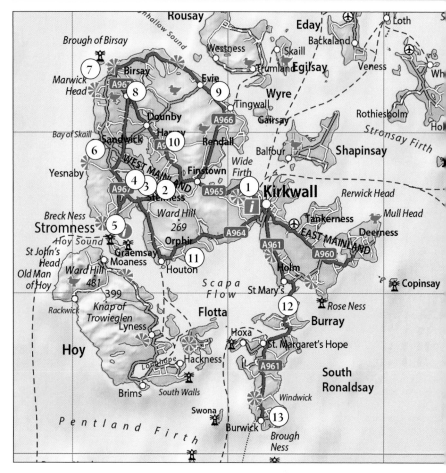

CULTURAL HERITAGE This itinerary covers the main archaeological and historical sites on the Mainland. It really needs at least a couple of days, perhaps combined with some of the suggested bird watching sites.

These sites are absolutely essential visits to see a good cross section of Orkney's monuments. Military installations from WWI and WWI are covered in Itinerary #18, while Natural heritage tours are covered in Itinerary #20 Summer and #21 Winter.

Please note that Skara Brae particularly can become congested in

the main season, especially when cruise ships are in. At such times it is best to arrive early or late in the day. During the long days of summer all of the unmanned sites are best appreciated in morning or evening light.

Maeshowe operates a timed hourly visits system which need to be booked in advance on the HES website. Opening hours should be checked, especially between October and March, when some sites are closed, and others have restricted hours. Some of the places which are seasonally closed may be visited by prior arrangement.

ORKNEY CULTURE	
1. Kirkwall	12
St Magnus Cathedral	14
Orkney Museum	12
2. Maeshowe	30
3. Standing Stones	28
4. Ring of Brodgar	24
5. Stromness Museum	12
Pier Arts Centre	12
6. Skara Brae	22
7. Brough of Birsay	34
8. Kirbuster Museum	39
9. Broch of Gurness	40
10. Corrigall Museum	39
11. Orphir Round Kirk	37
12. Italian Chapel	54
13. Tomb of the Eagles	56

ORDNANCE SURVEY 1:50,000 AND 1:25,000 MAPS OF ORKNEY

OS Landranger Map 6	Orkney - Mainland	OS Landranger Map 7	Orkney - Southern Isles
OS Explorer Map 463	Orkney - West Mainland	OS Explorer Map 461	Orkney - East Mainland

19. Cultural Heritage Tour

This long day out can be started at any point en route. Maeshowe tours must be prebooked. Opening times should be checked to avoid disappointment. The total distance is up to 160km (100mi) and the time is about 8 hours, excluding teabreaks and lunch. There are convenient public toilets at or near many of the suggested sites.

All of the places here are well signposted, so driving directions have not been included. By careful planning the crowds can be avoided, and the best viewing times chosen. The stars relate only to how essential the visit is on a first trip to Orkney. They do not imply any rating beyond that.

1. Kirkwall (page 12) has many place of interest, with *****St Magnus Cathedral** (page 14, *opening hours, no charge*) an essential visit on even the shortest of tours. ***Orkney Museum** (page 12, *opening hours, no charge*) is across the road from the Cathedral and provides a very good introduction to Orkney's cultural heritage (0km, 0mi, 60min).

2. *****Maeshowe (page 30, *opening hours, hourly tours from Visitor Centre, admission charge, online booking required*) should preferably be visited on the first tour of the day. In midwinter 1400 is best, in midsummer there are evening openings. Other visits can be timed to suit (16km, 10mi, 60min).

3. ***The Standing Stones of Stenness (page 28, *open at all times, no charge*) are most impressive in early morning or evening light. If time allows also visit the nearby **Barnhouse Village**. *****The Ness of Brodgar** should not be missed if excavation work is in progress (2km, 1.5mi, 30min).

4. *****Ring of Brodgar (page 24, *open at all times, no charge*) has a large carpark. Even if time is limited a walk around the stones is completely essential. Again they are at their best in morning or evening light (1.5km, 1mi, 30min).

5. Stromness (page 42) has limited parking spaces. On a short visit use the carpark next to the ferry terminal (fee payable). ***The Pier Arts Centre** (page 42, *opening hours, no charge*) has a permanent display as well as a programme of exhibitions. ***Stromness Museum** (page 12, *opening hours,*

admission charge) has exhibits which are complimentary to the Orkney Museum. Both could be visited during this tour, or during a visit to the town itself. Nearby ***Unstan Chambered Cairn** is similar to the Tomb of the Eagles and should be visited if there is not time to reach the latter (10km, 6mi, 60).

6. *****Skara Brae (page 22, *opening hours, admission charge, joint ticketing with Skaill House*) is considered by many to be the Jewel in the Crown of Orkney's archaeology. It is certainly an essential visit. ****Skaill House** (page 38, *opening hours, admission charge, joint ticketing with Skara Brae*) is adjacent, and is the only such house in Orkney open to the public (10km, 6mi, 90min for both).

7. ****The Brough of Birsay (page 34, *open at all times but access depends on the tide, no charge*) is a complete contrast to Skara Brae in that the Norse buildings can be entered and studied. Puffins may be seen here in summer (10km, 6mi, 60min).

8. **Kirbuster Museum (page 39, *opening hours, no charge*) is an interesting 19th century farm which can be visited en route (5km, 3.5mi, 30min).

9. *****The Broch of Gurness (page 40, *opening hours, admission charge*) is the best-preserved of about 100 such structures in Orkney. The tower, surrounding village and ramparts can all be explored. It is highly rated by children (14km, 9mi, 60min).

10. **Corrigall Farm Museum (page 39, *opening hours, no charge*) is a late 19th century farm, complete with animals and many artefacts. It is typical of the period (13km, 8.5mi, 30min).

11. **Orphir Round Kirk (*open at all times, no charge*) is a 12th century church. Nearby are remains of a Norse farm (32km, 20mi, 30min).

12. *****The Italian Chapel (page 54, *opening hours, no charge*) on Lamb Holm in Holm was built in WWII by Italian prisoners of war. It is an essential visit, not to be missed on any account (24km, 16mi, 60min return to Kirkwall).

13. ****Tomb of the Eagles (page 56, *opening hours, admission charge*) at the south end of South Ronaldsay is, along with its museum, one of the most impressive chambered cairns in Orkney. The drive and walk make it a fairly long visit (40km, 24mi, 100min return to Italian Chapel).

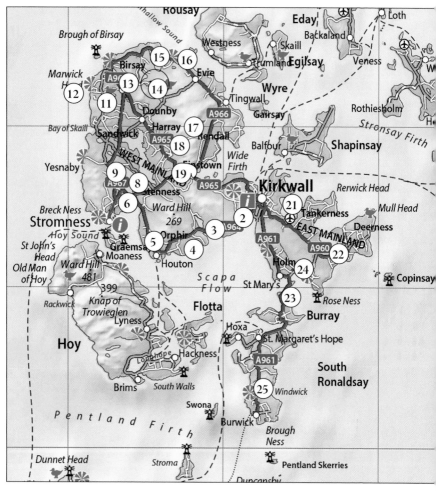

NATURAL HERITAGE IN SUMMER

Orkney abounds with breeding birds from late April until early August. This tour of the Mainland takes in most of the best sites and can be done in one longish day. Although here starting in Kirkwall, it can be joined at any point.

Most of Orkney's breeding species of waders, waterfowl, seabirds and raptors may be seen, as well as smaller species. A cross section of habitats, including beaches, headlands, cliffs, farmland, wetland, lochs and hills is suggested.

There are many options for tea-breaks and lunch in summer with several cafes and hotels. On a nice day a picnic is recommended. The route passes several shops along the way to stock up on supplies.

With the long hours of daylight, early morning can be an especially good time to see and hear the birds. The plaintive calls of the Curlew, Red-throated Diver and Lapwings carry far on a calm morning. Hen Harriers and Short-eared Owls silently quarter the verges and ditches for voles. The cliffs ledges have many auks.

THE ORKNEY GUIDE BOOK 4th EDITION

Orkney Natural Heritage i covered in detail in the Orkne Guide Book. Topics include Geology, Climate, Seabirds Landbirds, Waders, Waterfow Migrants, Winter Visitors Orkney Bird Names, Flora Orkney Plant Names, Seashore Land Fauna, Marine Fauna insects and Orkney Anima Names. Details of natur reserves and other places to vie wildlife are given throughout.

ORDNANCE SURVEY 1:50,000 AND 1:25,000 MAPS OF ORKNEY			
OS Landranger Map 6	Orkney - Mainland	OS Landranger Map 7	Orkney - Southern Isles
OS Explorer Map 463	Orkney - West Mainland	OS Explorer Map 461	Orkney - East Mainland

20. Natural Heritage Tour In Summer

This long day out can be started at any point. It is best to try to get to the beaches towards low tide. The total distance is up to 160km (100mi) and the time is about 8 hours, excluding teabreaks and lunch. Stromness and Skara Brae are good places for stops. There are convenient public toilets at many of the suggested sites.

2. Scapa Beach (page 13) From Kirkwall take the A963 south and turn off onto the B9148, then the B9053 at Scapa Bay. Scan tideline for waders. Also check shore on road to pier (3km, 2mi, 20min).

3. Hobbister RSPB Reserve Follow the A964 to Hobbister RSPB Reserve. From the carpark explore the various tracks (6km, 4mi, 30min).

4. Waulkmill Bay can be reached from the RSPB Reserve by path or by road, parking near the toilets. Take the steps to the beach. Skaith is a saltmarsh at the head of the bay (1.5km, 1mi, 30min).

5. Scorradale Carry on west on the A964, turn right uphill at Scorradale for a fine viewpoint (7km, mi, drive through).

6. Brig o' Waithe (page 42) Rejoin the A964 at Clestrain. Stop at the carpark the Brig of Waithe, where Stenness Loch drains into the sea. Heron, waders, waterfowl, Common Seals, saltmarsh plants (8km, 5mi, 30min).

8. Bridge of Brodgar (page 28) is a prime place to see breeding waterfowl, Mute Swans and various waders (4km, 2.5mi, drive through).

9. Brodgar Pools RSPB Reserve (page 24) Park in the Ring of Brodgar carpark off the B9055. Scan the wetland area northwest of the stones for waterfowl and waders(1.5km, 1mi, 30min).

11. Loons Hide RSPB (page 36) Continue northwest on the B9055, bear right onto the A967 to Twatt, then turn off left at the old church for the Loons Hide. Waterfowl, waders, raptors and passerines may all be seen (14km, 9mi, 30min).

12. Marwick Head (page 36) Turn right onto the B9056 and follow the sign for Marwick Head. Walk up the track to the Kitchener Memorial to see the huge seabird colony on the cliffs and Gannets offshore (2.5km, 1.5mi, 30min).

13. Durkadale RSPB (page 36) Return to the B9056 and return to Twatt on the A986, turn left onto the Hundland Road, then keep right at

the junction to reach the RSPB Reserve (9km, 5mi, 30min).

14. Hillside Road (page 36) Carry on southeast to the B9057, bear left for Evie on the Hillside Road, looking out for raptors. (8km, 5mi, drive through).

15. Burgar Hill Hide (page 36) Turn left onto the A966 and left to the signposted hide at Lowrie's Water on Burgar Hill to see Red-throated Divers (2km, 1.5mi, 30min).

16. Sands of Aikerness (page 40) Return to the A966 and head southeast to Aikerness, follow signs for Broch of Gurness. Scan the shoreline and Eynhallow Sound (3km, 2mi, 30min).

17. Cottasgarth RSPB Follow the A966 towards Finstown, turn off right towards Cottasgarth to see Hen Harriers and other raptors from the new bird hide (8km, 5mi, 30min).

18. Lyde Road Continue west along the Lyde Road looking out for raptors and waders, then take the A986 and A965 to Finstown (11km, 8mi, drive through).

19. Binscarth Plantation Park in Finstown and follow the signposted footpath to the woods. If time permits continue along the footpath to the Refuge Corner via Wasdale Loch. Return to Kirkwall on the A965 (10km, 7mi, 30-60min).

21. Mill Sands (page 53) Follow the A960 past the airport, turn left to Tankerness, then right at an old mill. The sands ebb dry (7km, 5mi, 30min).

22. St Peter's Pool (page 53) Return to the A960 at the community hall and turn left. The Bay of Suckquoy and St Peter's Pool are both prime wader spots (12km, 7.5mi, 30min).

23. Churchill Barriers (page 54) Turn left off the A960 at the school towards Holm. Holm Sound can be scanned from the B9052 and the Churchill Barriers for seaducks. This is also a good place to see terns in flight (16km, 10mi, 60min).

24. St Mary's and Graemeshall Lochs (page 53) is on the west side of St Mary's, while Graemeshall Loch is to the east off the B9052 (2km, 1.5mi, 30min). Return to Kirkwall on the A961 (10km, 7mi, 30min).

25. Olav's Wood at Windwick in South Ronaldsay is a mixed woodland and haven for wildlife. It follows the Oback Burn. Access is off the A961, signposted for Windwick. A signposted gate is the entry point.

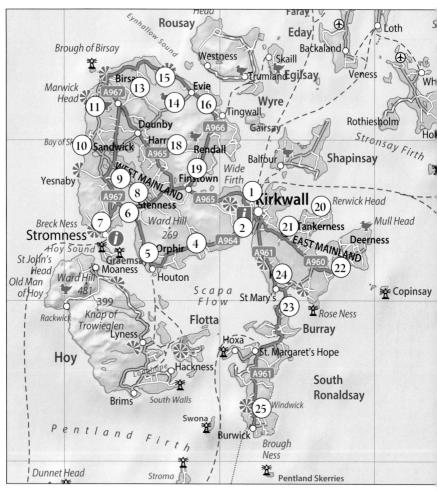

Natural Heritage in Winter

Orkney presents a quite different selection of birds in winter, with many species which breed further north passing through on their way north in spring or south in autumn. Many also spend the winter here. A day out at this time of year can easily result in seeing up to 100 species, especially with some advance intelligence.

Approximate distances and times are indicated. In many cases the car will make a very good hide, but short walks are needed at most of the sites. A start at around 09:00 is needed to take advantage of the limited light in midwinter.

Out of season opportunities for tea and lunchbreaks are limited. Stromness, Dounby and Skara Brae all have year round cafés or hotels. Opening hours should be checked to avoid disappointment. In any case, with only six hours of daylight, a flask of coffee and sandwiches is perhaps quicker.

Orkney frequently offers a wild and raw aspect of nature during the winter especially in storms.

The Orkney Guide Book 4th edition

Orkney Natural Heritage is covered in detail in the Orkney Guide Book. Topics include Geology, Climate, Seabirds, Landbirds, Waders, Waterfowl, Migrants, Winter Visitors, Orkney Bird Names, Flora, Orkney Plant Names, Seashore, Land Fauna, Marine Fauna, insects and Orkney Animal Names. Details of nature reserves and other places to view wildlife are given throughout.

ORDNANCE SURVEY 1:50,000 AND 1:25,000 MAPS OF ORKNEY

OS Landranger Map 6 Orkney - Mainland OS Landranger Map 7 Orkney - Southern Isles
OS Explorer Map 463 Orkney - West Mainland OS Explorer Map 461 Orkney - East Mainland

---

21. NATURAL HERITAGE TOUR IN WINTER

This long day out can be started at any point. It is best to try to get to the beaches towards low tide. The total distance is up to 160km (100mi) and the time is about 8 hours, excluding teabreaks and lunch. Stromness and Skara Brae are good places for stops. There are convenient public toilets at many of the suggested sites.

1. Kirkwall Harbour & Peedie Sea (page 12) The shore on both sides of the pier as well as Kirkwall bay should be checked. Park opposite Tescos and walk around the Peedie Sea. The part nearest the road is usually best (0km, 0mi, 30min).
2. Scapa Beach (page 13) From Kirkwall take the A963 south and turn off onto the B9148, then the B9053 at Scapa Bay. Scan tideline for waders. Also check shore on road to pier (3km, 2mi, 20min).
4. Waulkmill Bay can be reached from #3 or by road, parking near the toilets. Take the steps to the beach. Skaith is a saltmarsh at the head of the bay (1.5km, 1mi, 30min).
5. Scorradale Carry on west on the A964, turn right uphill at Scorradale for a fine viewpoint (7km, 4.5mi, drive through).
6. Brig o' Waithe (page 42) Rejoin the A964 at Clestrain. Stop at the carpark at the Brig of Waithe, where Stenness Loch drains into the sea. Heron, Common Seals, saltmarsh plants (8km, 5mi, 30min).
7. Stromness Harbour (page 42) Park in the long stay carpark. The head of the bay, labelled "Hamnavoe" on the map is best when the tide is out. Also scan the pier area (3km, 2mi, 30min).
8. Bridge of Brodgar (page 24) is a prime place to see breeding waterfowl, Mute Swans and various waders (4km, 2.5mi, drive through).
9. Brodgar Pools RSPB Reserve (page 24) Park in the Ring of Brodgar carpark off the B9055. Scan the wetland area northwest of the stones for waterfowl and waders(1.5km, 1mi, 30min).
10. Loch of Skaill (page 36) Park near the lochside and look for migrant and over wintering waders, waterfowl and gulls (6km, 4mi, 30min).
11. Loons Hide RSPB (page 36) Continue northwest on the B9055, bear right onto the A967 to Twatt, then turn off left at the old church for the

Loons Hide. Waterfowl, waders, raptors and passerines may all be seen (14km, 9mi, 30min).
13. Durkadale RSPB (page 36) Return to the B9056 and to Twatt on the A986, turn left onto the Hundland Road, then keep right at the junction to reach the RSPB Reserve (9km, 5mi, 30min).
14. Hillside Road (page 36) Carry on southeast to the B9057, bear left for Evie on the Hillside Road, looking out for raptors. (8km, 5mi, drive through).
15. Burgar Hill Hide (page 36) Turn left onto the A966 and left to the signposted hide on Burgar Hill to see Red-throated Divers (2km, 1.5mi, 30min).
16. Sands of Aikerness (page 40) Return to the A966 and head southeast to Aikerness, follow signs for Broch of Gurness. Scan the shoreline and Eynhallow Sound (3km, 2mi, 30min).
18. Lyde Road Continue west along the Lyde Road looking out for raptors and waders, then take the A986 and A965 to Finstown (11km, 7.5mi, drive through).
19. Finstown Ouse Follow a side road from the village, then continue on this road and return to Finstown on the A966. Go back to Kirkwall on the A965 (10km, 7mi, drive through).
20. Rerwick Head (page 53) Return to the old mill, turn right and follow the road all the way to Rerwick Head for seaducks and divers (5km, 3.5mi, 30min).
21. Mill Sands (page 53) Follow the A960 past the airport, turn left to Tankerness, then right at an old mill. The sands ebb dry (7km, 5mi, 30min).
22. St Peter's Pool (page 53) Return to the A960 at the community hall and turn left. The Bay of Suckquoy and St Peter's Pool are both prime wader spots (12km, 7.5mi, 30min).
23. Churchill Barriers (page 54) Turn left off the A960 at the school towards Holm. Holm Sound can be scanned from the B9052 and the Churchill Barriers for seaducks and divers (8km, 5mi, 30min).
24. St Mary's Loch (page 53) is on the west side of St Mary's and usually holds good numbers of waterfowl (1km, 0.8mi, 15min). Return to Kirkwall on the A961 (10km, 7mi, 10min).
25. Olav's Wood at Windwick in South Ronaldsay is a mixed woodland and haven for wildlife. It follows the Oback Burn. Access is off the A961, signposted for Windwick. A signposted gate is the entry point.

Orkney Today - Black Kye, Wind Turbines and Cruise Ship

BIBLIOGRAPHY

BOOKS ON ORKNEY

A small selection of useful books on Orkney is listed below. The most comprehensive and up to date Guide Book is the new edition of the Orkney Guide Book. This 624 page book covers every aspect of the islands in depth and the latest edition was published in 2012. It includes a very full bibliography of sources. Orkney bookshops include The Orcadian and David Spence in Kirkwall, Stromness Books and Prints, as well as outlets at Skara Brae, Maeshowe Visitor Centre, Skaill House, Orkney Fossil and Heritage Centre and the Tomb of the Eagles.

The Orkney Guide Book, 4th edition Charles Tait		Charles Tait	2012
Orkney	Howie Firth	Robert Hale	2013

HISTORY & ARCHAEOLOGY

Between the Wind and the Water	Caroline Wickham-Jones	Windgather	2006
The New History of Orkney	William PL Thomson	Mercat Press	2001
Last Dawn, Royal Oak Tragedy	David Turner	Argyll Publishing	2009
Orkney Land and People	William PL Thomson	Orcadian	2008
The Kirkwall Ba'	John DM Robertson	Dunedin Academic Press	2005

LOCAL GUIDE BOOKS

The local Guide Books produced by Historic Scotland and others are all worth buying. These include: Orkney's Italian Chapel, Skara Brae, Maeshowe, Brochs of Gurness & Midhowe, Bishop's and Earl's Palaces, St Magnus Cathedral and the Tomb of the Eagles.

Walking on Orkney & Shetland	Graham Uney	Cicerone	2009

NORSE SAGAS

Orkneyinga Saga	trans. H Pálsson & P Edwards	Hogarth	1978
Magnus' Saga	trans. H Pálsson & P Edwards	Perpetua	1987

RECENT MILITARY HISTORY

Orkney at War Vol 1 World War I	Geoffrey Stell	Orcadian	2011
Cox's Navy	Tony Booth	Pen & Sword	2005
Scapa Flow	Ludwig von Reuter	Wordsmith	2005
Scapa Flow Defences 1914-45	Angus Konstam	Osprey	2009

NATURAL HISTORY

Collins Bird Guide	Mullarney, Svensson, Zetterstrom & Grant	HarperCollins	2000
Scottish Birds: Culture & Tradition	Robin Hull	Mercat Press	2001
Orkney Bird Report	eds Booth, Cuthbert & Meek		1983-2016
Guide to Sea & Shore Life	Gibson, Hextall & Rogers	Oxford	2001
The Natural History of Seals	W Nigel Bonner	Helm	1989
Sea Mammals of the World	Folkens, Reeves et al	A&C Black	2002
Butterflies & Moths	Sterry & Mackay	Dorling Kindersley	2004
Wild Flowers of Britain & Ireland	Blamey, Fitter & Fitter	A&C Black	2003
Plants & People in Ancient Scotland	Dickson & Dickson	Tempus	2000
Scottish Wild Plants	Lusby & Wright	Mercat Press	2001

MAPS

OS Landranger Map 5	Orkney – Northern Isles	Ordnance Survey	2008
OS Landranger Map 6	Orkney - Mainland	Ordnance Survey	2007
OS Landranger Map 7	Orkney – Southern Isles	Ordnance Survey	2008
OS Explorer Map 461	Orkney - East Mainland	Ordnance Survey	2007
OS Explorer Map 462	Orkney – Hoy, South Walls & Flotta	Ordnance Survey	2010
OS Explorer Map 463	Orkney – West Mainland	Ordnance Survey	2007
OS Explorer Map 464	Orkney – Westray, Papa Westray, Rousay, Egilsay & Wyre	Ordnance Survey	2007
OS Explorer Map 465	Orkney – Sanday, Eday, N Ronaldsay & Stronsay	Ordnance Survey	2007

Total eclipse of the sun, March 20th 2015

INDEX

CHARLES TAIT
GUIDE BOOKS

Charles Tait Guide Books

Orkney Guide Book, 4ᵗʰ ed (656p)
ISBN 9780951785980 (£24.95)
Orkney Peedie Guide, 4ᵗʰ ed revised (144p)
ISBN 9781909036000 (£9.95)
Outer Hebrides Guide Book, 3ʳᵈ ed rev (256p)
ISBN 9780951785997 (£12.95)
Shetland Guide Book, 2ⁿᵈ ed (176p)
ISBN 9780951785942 (£12.95)
North Highlands Guide Book, 1ˢᵗ ed (400p)
ISBN 9780951785966 (£14.95)
Isle of Skye Guide Book, 1ˢᵗ ed (256p)
ISBN 9780951785973 (£12.95)
North Coast 500 Guide Book, 1ˢᵗ ed (256p)
ISBN 9781909036604 (£12.95)
Scapa Flow Guide Book, 1ˢᵗ ed (144p)
ISBN 9781909036024 (£9.95) - 2018

Charles Tait Miniguides

Orkney Miniguide, 2ⁿᵈ edition (64p)
ISBN 9781909036154 (£4.95)
Heart of Neolithic Orkney Miniguide, 1ˢᵗ ed (96p)
ISBN 9781909036123 (£6.95)

Charles Tait Dorset Guide Books

Dorset Guide Book, 1ˢᵗ ed (384p)
ISBN 9781909036314 (£14.95)
West Dorset Guide, 1ˢᵗ ed (128p)
ISBN 9781909036321 (£6.95)
Purbeck Guide Book, 1ˢᵗ ed (96p)
ISBN 9781909036338 (£6.95)

Charles Tait Photographer & Travel Writer

Charles Tait has been publishing guide books since 1991, with nearly 100,000 sold. All are photographed, researched, written and designed by the author and lavishly illustrated by his photographs, with maps, old prints and other images. His strict policy of only writing about places he has visited gives this series an authenticity often lacking elsewhere. The guides have a common layout and are authoritative, yet easy to read and use.

Kelton, St Ola, Orkney KW15 1TR
Tel 01856 873738   charles.tait@zetnet.co.uk   c h a r l e s - t a i t . c o . u k